Master the Year 3 basics with CGP!

This superb CGP Foundation Targeted Question Book is perfect for helping pupils get to grips with Maths in Year 3.

There's a huge range of questions on all the most important Maths skills, carefully written to build pupils' confidence. Answers are included at the back.

And there's more! We've included practice tests at the start and end of the book — ideal for keeping track of progress. Enjoy!

What CGP is all about

Our sole aim here at CGP is to produce the highest quality books — carefully written, immaculately presented and dangerously close to being funny.

Then we work our socks off to get them out to you — at the cheapest possible prices.

Contents

About This Book 1

Year Two Objectives Test 2

Section One – Number and Place Value

Place Value 6
Reading and Writing Numbers 7
Counting in Multiples 8
10 or 100 More or Less 9
Ordering and Comparing Numbers 10
Partitioning 12
Numbers on Scales 14
Solving Number Problems 16

Section Two – Calculations

Mental Addition 18
Mental Subtraction 19
Written Addition 20
Written Subtraction 21
The 3, 4 and 8 Times Tables 22
Using Times Tables Facts 23
Estimating and Checking 25
Solving Calculation Problems 26

Section Three – Fractions

Counting in Tenths 28
Equivalent Fractions 29
Ordering Fractions 30
Adding and Subtracting Fractions 32
Fractions of Amounts 34
Solving Fraction Problems 36

Section Four – Measurement

- Length, Mass and Volume 38
- Perimeter 40
- Money 42
- Clocks 43
- Time Problems 44

Section Five – Geometry

- 2D Shapes 46
- 3D Shapes 48
- Angles and Lines 50

Section Six – Statistics

- Tables 52
- Bar Charts 53
- Pictograms 54
- Interpreting Tables and Charts 55

Year Three Objectives Test 56

Answers 60

Published by CGP

Editors:
Martha Bozic, Katie Fernandez, Josie Gilbert, Rachel Hickman,
Duncan Lindsay, Ali Palin, Tamara Sinivassen.

ISBN: 978 1 78908 043 8

With thanks to Samuel Mann for the proofreading.
With thanks to Emily Smith for the copyright research.

Printed by Elanders Ltd, Newcastle upon Tyne.

Clipart from Corel®

Based on the classic CGP style created by Richard Parsons.

Text, design, layout and original illustrations © Coordination Group Publications Ltd. (CGP) 2022

All rights reserved.

Photocopying this book is not permitted, even if you have a CLA licence.
Extra copies are available from CGP with next day delivery • 0800 1712 712 • www.cgpbooks.co.uk

About This Book

This Book is Full of Year 3 Maths Questions

You'll learn a lot of new maths in Year 3.

This foundation book has questions on all the maths for Year 3 at a slightly easier level — so it's perfect if you're getting to grips with the Year 3 topics.

It matches our Year 3 Study Book.
This can help you if you get stuck.

The answers to all of the questions are at the back of this book.

This book covers the Attainment Targets for Year 3 of the National Curriculum.

There are Two Objectives Tests in This Book

The one at the front of the book is to test that you remember the maths you learnt in Year 2.

The test at the back of the book is to see how well you know the maths in this book.

The questions in each test cover a mix of different topics and get trickier as you work through the test.

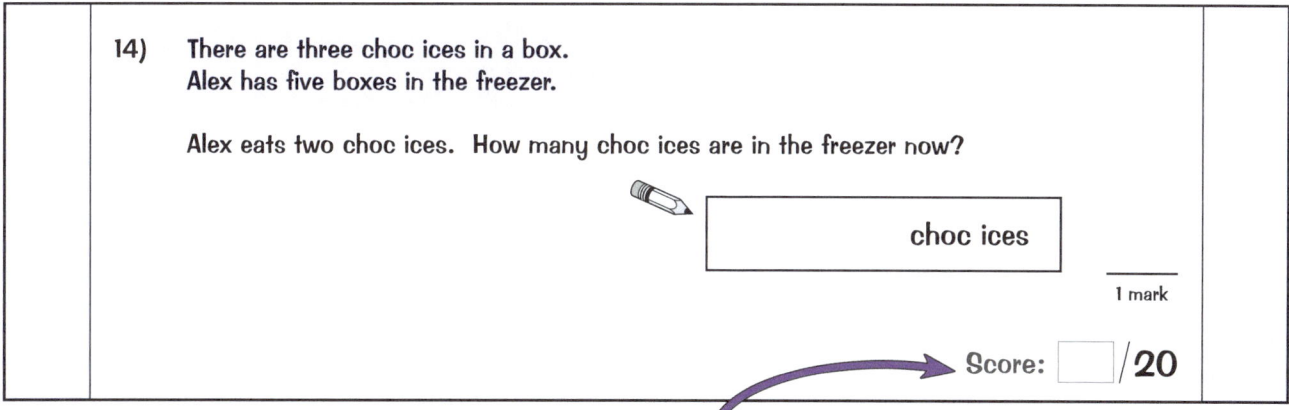

You can add up your score at the end to see how many you got right.

Use the Tick Boxes to Say How You're Doing

At the end of each topic, you'll see faces like the ones at the bottom of this page.
Tick the one that matches how confident you feel with the questions on the page.

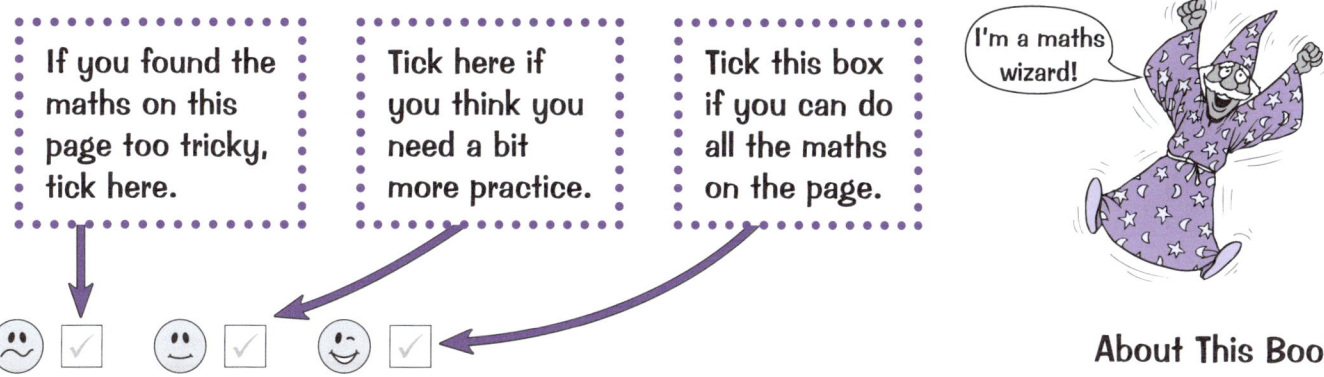

Year Two Objectives Test

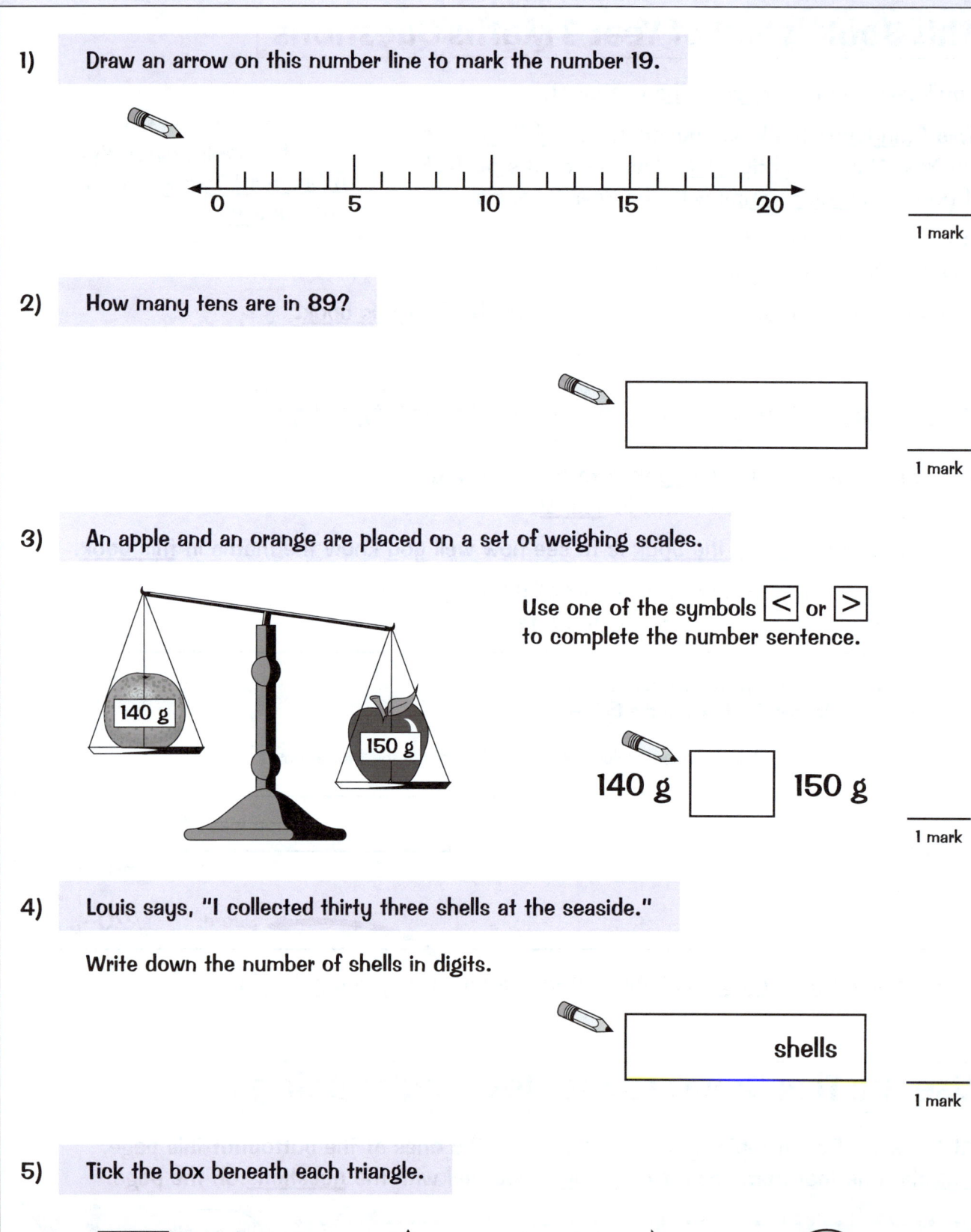

1) Draw an arrow on this number line to mark the number 19.

   1 mark

2) How many tens are in 89?

   1 mark

3) An apple and an orange are placed on a set of weighing scales.

   Use one of the symbols < or > to complete the number sentence.

   140 g ☐ 150 g

   1 mark

4) Louis says, "I collected thirty three shells at the seaside."

   Write down the number of shells in digits.

   _____ shells

   1 mark

5) Tick the box beneath each triangle.

   1 mark

Year Two Objectives Test

Year Two Objectives Test

6) Circle the bigger number in each pair.

✏ 35   or   90   ✏ 56   or   81

1 mark

7) Suzette asked her friends and family what their favourite method to send a message is.

She draws a tally chart to show her results.

Method	Tally
Text message	⊞ I
Email	IIII
Post	⊞
Carrier pigeon	I

Which method is the most popular?

✏ [   ]

1 mark

How many people said post is their favourite method?

✏ [   ]

1 mark

8) Start at 10 and count up 3 steps of 5. What number do you reach?

✏ [   ]

1 mark

9) Calculate:

✏ 8 × 2 = [   ]   ✏ 5 × 10 = [   ]

2 marks

10) Maxine has been to **48** yoga classes.

Sharon has been to 6 more classes than Maxine.
How many classes has Sharon been to?

classes

1 mark

Carl has been to 10 fewer classes than Maxine.
How many classes has Carl been to?

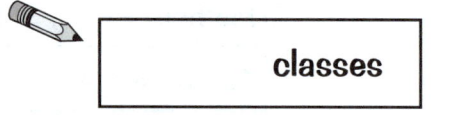

classes

1 mark

11) Write down the time shown on the clock in words.

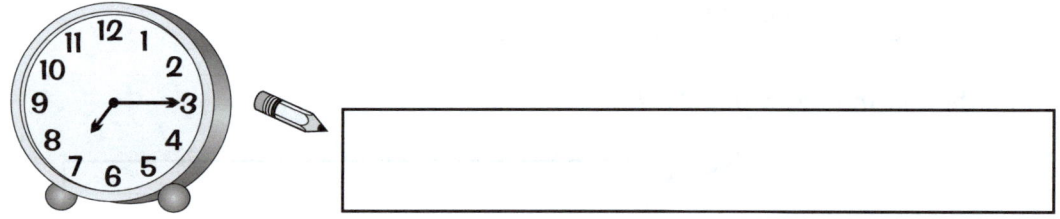

1 mark

12) Yu is following these directions to find his friend's house.

*Go **forward**, take the **second left**, then **turn right**.
My house is at the end of the street, on the **right**.*

Three routes (A, B and C) are drawn below.

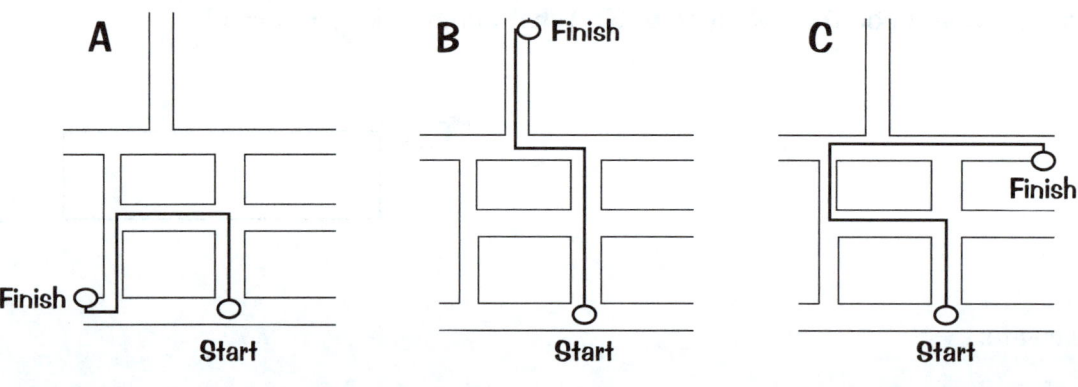

Write the letter of the route that matches the directions.

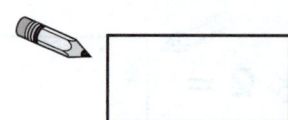

1 mark

Year Two Objectives Test

13) Work out the answer to this sum.

5 + 8 + 2 =

1 mark

14) Draw lines to match each shape with the words that describe it.

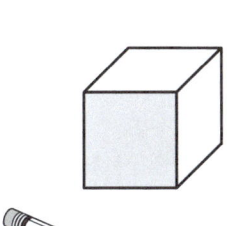 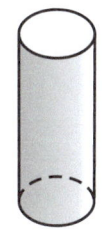  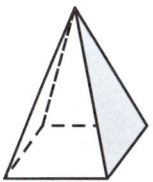

6 square faces   5 vertices and 5 faces   0 vertices and 0 edges   0 vertices and 2 edges

2 marks

15) A farmer has 8 sheep. Some of them are in a pen.

Circle the fraction below that represents the fraction of sheep in the pen.

$\frac{1}{4}$ $\frac{2}{4}$ $\frac{3}{4}$

1 mark

4 of the sheep are going to be sheared.
Fill in the box to show what fraction of the sheep will be sheared.

☐ / 2

1 mark

Score: ☐ /20

Section One — Number and Place Value

Place Value

1 Match each number to the digit in its 'ones' place.

The first one has been done for you.

248 ——————————— 7

307   0

972 ——————————— 8

720   2

2 marks

2 There are 5 tens in the number 250.

How many hundreds are there in 250? Circle the correct answer.

2   20   200

1 mark

3 Write down the digit in the 'tens' place for each of these numbers.

80   734

2 marks

4 Complete the sentence below.

The 4 in 412 is in the _____ place.

1 mark

5 Write down the value of 6 in the number 569.

1 mark

Section One — Number and Place Value

Reading and Writing Numbers

1 Fill in the missing digits to write these numbers in numerals.
The first one has been done for you.

four hundred and twenty eight   4 2 [8]

nine hundred and fifty nine   [ ] 5 [ ]

seven hundred and fifteen   [ ] [ ] 5

2 marks

2 Write down one hundred and three as a number.

1 mark

3 What is 846 in words?
Put a tick in the correct box.

[ ] eight hundred and four
[ ] eight hundred and forty six
[ ] four hundred and eighty six
[ ] eighty six

1 mark

4 Write down 362 in words.

1 mark

Section One — Number and Place Value

Counting in Multiples

1) Write down the first four multiples of 4.

Two have been done for you.

| 4 |, | |, | |, | 16 |

1 mark

2) Write down the first five multiples of 50.

Two have been done for you.

| 50 |, | 100 |, | |, | |, | |

1 mark

3) Write down the first five multiples of 8.

One has been done for you.

| |, | |, | 24 |, | |, | |

1 mark

4) Circle all the multiples of 100.

350   200   120   70   300   900

1 mark

5) Count up in multiples of 8 to fill in the boxes.

| 40 |, | |, | |

1 mark

Section One — Number and Place Value

10 or 100 More or Less

1) What number is 10 more than 51?

2) What number is 10 less than 334?

3) Circle the number that is 100 more than 540.

600   440   640   550   530

4) Write down the number that is one hundred less than nine hundred.

Write your answer in digits.

5) Circle the number that is 10 less than 109.

119   99   100   9

6) Count up in 10s to fill in the boxes.

870 , 880 , ___ , ___ , ___

Section One — Number and Place Value

Ordering and Comparing Numbers

1 Circle the larger number.

702   167

1 mark

2 Circle the smaller number.

351   349

1 mark

3 Write 'larger' or 'smaller' in the boxes to make these sentences correct.

578 is [   ] than 590.

421 is [   ] than 321.

2 marks

4 Put these numbers in order. Start with the smallest.

380   191   102

[   ]   [   ]   [   ]
smallest   largest

1 mark

5 Put these numbers in order. Start with the largest.

111   56   850   320

[   ] [   ] [   ] [   ]
largest   smallest

1 mark

Section One — Number and Place Value

Ordering and Comparing Numbers

6 Look at these numbers. Write > or < in the box.

981 ☐ 891

1 mark

7 Three apples and their masses are shown below.

141 g   167 g   145 g

Write down the mass of the heaviest apple.

☐ g

1 mark

8 Camilla, Josephine and Liam are each given a bag of coins. There are 68 coins in Camilla's bag, 301 coins in Josephine's bag and 97 coins in Liam's bag.

Who has the smallest number of coins?

☐

1 mark

9 Put a tick in the box next to the correct statement.

☐ 224 < 250

☐ 224 > 250

☐ 224 = 250

1 mark

Section One — Number and Place Value

Partitioning

1 Partition the following numbers.

Some of the boxes have been filled in for you.

220 = [200] + [   ]

1 mark

309 = [   ] + [9]

1 mark

870 = [800] + [   ]

1 mark

2 Fill in the totals.

500 + 80 = [   ]

1 mark

100 + 60 + 1 = [   ]

1 mark

3 Partition the following numbers into hundreds, tens and ones.

Some of the boxes have been filled in for you.

542 = [500] + [   ] + [   ]

1 mark

468 = [   ] + [60] + [   ]

1 mark

951 = [   ] + [   ] + [1]

1 mark

Section One — Number and Place Value

Partitioning

4 Partition the following numbers into hundreds, tens and ones.

617 = ☐ + ☐ + ☐

1 mark

999 = ☐ + ☐ + ☐

1 mark

5 Bjorn wants to work out 27 + 112.

Fill in the boxes to partition 27 and 112.

27 = ☐ + ☐   112 = ☐ + ☐ + ☐

2 marks

Use your partitions to work out 27 + 112.

☐

1 mark

6 Use partitioning to find the answer to 184 + 13.

☐

2 marks

7 A farmer has 500 sheep in his field, 30 sheep in his pen and 2 sheep in his garden. How many sheep does he have in total?

☐

1 mark

Numbers on Scales

1 Draw an arrow pointing to 16 cm on the ruler below.

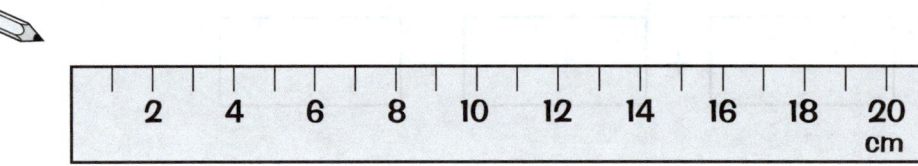

1 mark

2 What temperature is shown on this thermometer?

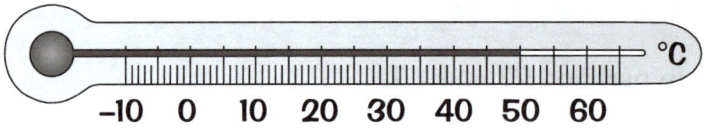

 °C

1 mark

3 What is the height of the snail?

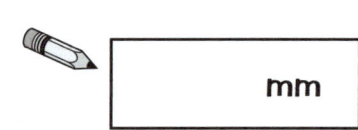 mm

1 mark

4 Draw an arrow pointing to 7 cm on the ruler below.

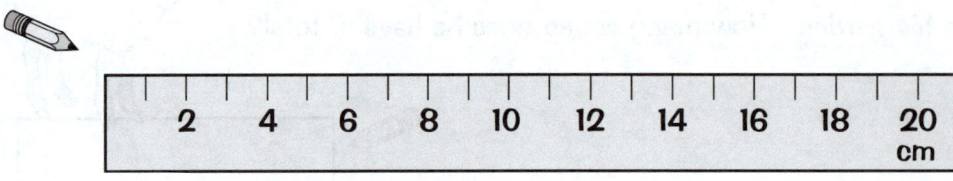

1 mark

Section One — Number and Place Value

Numbers on Scales

5 How many litres of water are in this tank?

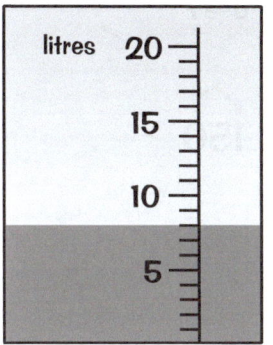

litres

1 mark

6 Write down the length that the arrow is pointing at.

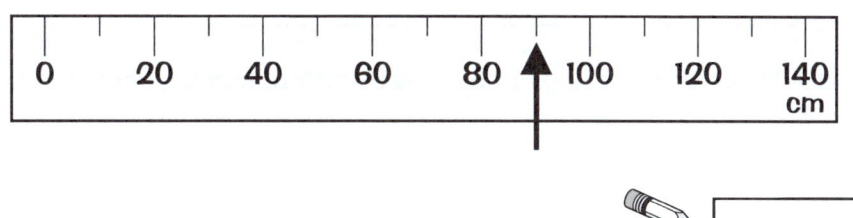

cm

1 mark

7 A bunch of bananas is hung on some weighing scales.

How much does the bunch of bananas weigh?

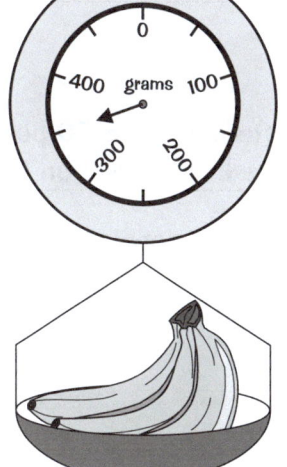

g

1 mark

Section One — Number and Place Value

Solving Number Problems

1 A beaver builds a dam using one hundred and fifty pieces of wood.

How many pieces of wood does the beaver use?
Circle the correct answer.

50   100   150   200

1 mark

2 Here are the number of days that it rained in one year in two different cities.

| Beachville | 251 |
| Swamponia | 229 |

Partition the number of rainy days in Beachville into hundreds, tens and ones.

☐ + ☐ + ☐

1 mark

Circle the name of the city that had the most rainy days.

Beachville   Swamponia

1 mark

3 Donatella is given 50 pennies for every day that she makes her bed. She makes her bed on 3 days.

How many pennies does Donatella get in total?

☐ pennies

1 mark

Section One — Number and Place Value

Solving Number Problems

4 A microwave costs £286 on a market stall.
The same microwave costs £100 more in a shop.

How much does the microwave cost in the shop?

£ _____

1 mark

5 A treasure hunter is following these instructions.

> Walk three hundred metres south
> Then ten metres west
> Then nine metres north

What is the total distance that she must walk?

_____ metres

1 mark

6 The temperature in a science lab is 0 °C.

The temperature increases by 8 °C every hour.
Write the temperature after four hours on the thermometer.

_____ °C

1 mark

Section One — Number and Place Value

Section Two — Calculations

Mental Addition

This page is on mental addition, so you need to do these sums in your head.

1 Calculate these sums.

456 + 2

671 + 5

202 + 9

1 mark (×3)

2 Match up the sums with their answers.

One has been done for you.

231 + 50	198
330 + 20	281
518 + 80	598
128 + 70	350

(231 + 50 is matched to 281)

2 marks

3 Work out the answers to these additions.

462 + 500

148 + 800

1 mark (×2)

4 Write a number in each box to make these sums correct.

564 + ☐ = 571   219 + ☐ = 420

2 marks

Mental Subtraction

This page is on <u>mental</u> subtraction, so you need to do these calculations in your head.

1) Calculate the answers to these subtractions.

845 − 3

158 − 5

747 − 8

1 mark

1 mark

1 mark

2) Match up the calculations with their answers.

One has been done for you.

905 − 100   155

455 − 300   58

558 − 500   805

875 − 700   175

2 marks

3) Fill in the boxes to make these calculations correct.

265 − 20 =   754 −   = 724

2 marks

4) What do you get when you subtract forty from 751?

1 mark

Section Two — Calculations

Written Addition

1 Calculate the following.

Use the columns to help you.

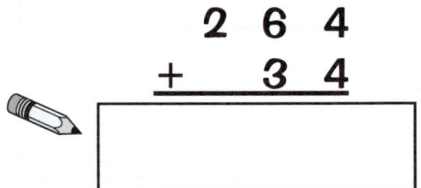
```
  2 6 4
+   3 4
```

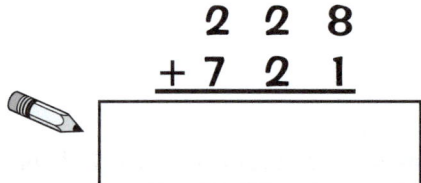
```
  3 2 1
+   5 8
```

2 marks

```
  4 7 3
+ 1 2 4
```

```
  2 2 8
+ 7 2 1
```

2 marks

2 Use a written method to work out 847 + 127.

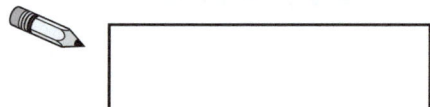

1 mark

3 Leila takes 785 steps to get from her house to her school.
She takes 43 steps to get from school to the park.

How many steps is this in total?

steps

1 mark

Section Two — Calculations

Written Subtraction

1) Carry out the following subtractions.

Use the columns to help you.

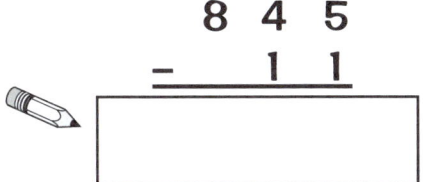
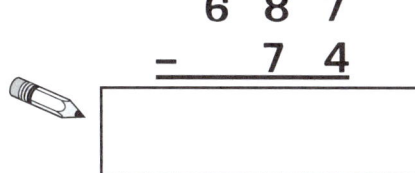

2 marks

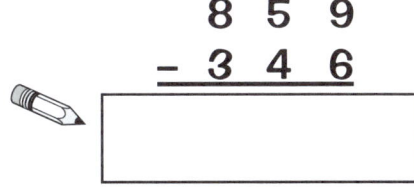
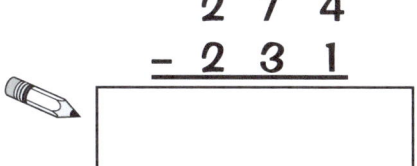

2 marks

2) Use a written method to work out 364 − 159.

1 mark

3) What is the answer to 426 − 286?

1 mark

Section Two — Calculations

The 3, 4 and 8 Times Tables

1 Fill in the boxes to make these calculations correct.

One of the boxes has been filled in for you.

4 + 4 + 4 = [3] × 4 = [ ]

1 mark

8 + 8 + 8 + 8 + 8 = [ ] × 8 = [ ]

1 mark

2 Use the times tables to calculate:

3 × 3 = [ ]

1 mark

6 × 4 = [ ]

1 mark

11 × 8 = [ ]

1 mark

3 Fill in the boxes to make these calculations correct.

[ ] × 8 = 64   5 × [ ] = 20

2 marks

4 A cat takes four naps each day. What is the total number of naps the cat takes in nine days?

[ ] naps

1 mark

Section Two — Calculations

Using Times Tables Facts

1) Calculate:

15 ÷ 3 = ☐   28 ÷ 7 = ☐

2 marks

2) Use the fact that 7 × 8 = 56 to do these calculations.

8 × 7 = ☐

1 mark

7 × 80 = ☐

1 mark

70 × 8 = ☐

1 mark

3) Fill in the boxes.

3 × 6 = ☐   30 × 6 = ☐

2 marks

4) Match up each calculation with its answer.

One has been done for you.

30 × 8   160
4 × 40   480
6 × 80   240
20 × 3   60

2 marks

Section Two — Calculations

Using Times Tables Facts

5 Work out the answers to these calculations.

36 ÷ 4 = [ ]

1 mark

360 ÷ 4 = [ ]

1 mark

6 Three people make a total of 90 jumpers.
They make the same number of jumpers each.

How many jumpers did each person make?

[ ] jumpers

1 mark

7 Fill in the boxes.

20 × 2 = [ ]   10 × 4 = [ ]

4 × 2 = [ ]   7 × 4 = [ ]

So 24 × 2 = [ ]   So 17 × 4 = [ ]

2 marks

8 Work out this division.

48 ÷ 3

[ ]

1 mark

Section Two — Calculations

Estimating and Checking

1 Here is a subtraction: 84 − 27 = 57.

Write an addition that uses the same numbers.

☐ + ☐ = ☐

1 mark

2 Gregory has worked out that 45 ÷ 3 = 15.

Fill in the box to make a calculation Gregory could use to check he's right.

15 × ☐ = 45

1 mark

3 Barack says, "12 + 29 = 41".

Circle a calculation you could use to estimate whether his answer is correct.

20 + 30   10 + 30   10 + 20   20 + 40

1 mark

4 Bobby's teacher asks him to calculate 101 ÷ 5.

Fill in the box to make a calculation that Bobby could use to estimate the answer.

☐ ÷ 5

1 mark

Bobby thinks that 101 ÷ 5 = 40. Explain how you know that Bobby is wrong.

1 mark

Section Two — Calculations

Solving Calculation Problems

1 280 trains pass through a station on Monday.
60 fewer trains pass through the station on Tuesday.

How many trains pass through the station on Tuesday?

_____ trains

1 mark

2 There are 33 children in Class 3 at Elaine's school.
There are a total of 146 children in the rest of the school.

How many children are there in total in the whole school?

_____ children

1 mark

3 Troy has 4 crayons. Skye has triple this amount.

How many crayons does Skye have?

_____ crayons

1 mark

4 Calculate three hundred and forty two plus four hundred and thirty nine.

_____

1 mark

Solving Calculation Problems

5 A total of 60 trees are planted in 3 parks.
The same number of trees are planted in each park.

How many trees are planted in each park?

[_____ trees]

1 mark

6 Farmer Frederic sells cabbages in boxes of eight.

Darcey buys 12 boxes. How many cabbages has she bought in total?

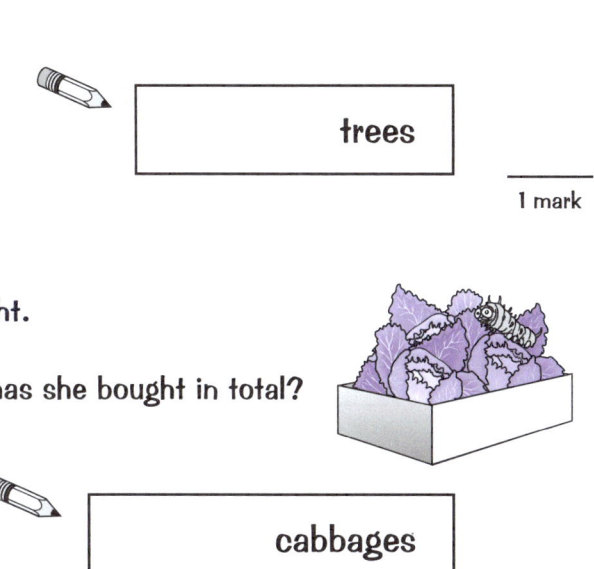

[_____ cabbages]

1 mark

Saul buys 16 cabbages. How many boxes has he bought?

[_____ boxes]

1 mark

7 Evie posts four letters each day.

She posts the first letters on Monday.
How many letters has she posted <u>in total</u> after posting Tuesday's letters?

[_____ letters]

1 mark

On which day does she post her 20th letter?

[_____]

1 mark

Section Two — Calculations

Section Three — Fractions

Counting in Tenths

1 Fill in the boxes.

$1 \div 10 = \dfrac{\boxed{}}{10}$

$\boxed{} \div 10 = \dfrac{6}{10}$

2 marks

2 Circle the rectangle that is $\dfrac{3}{10}$ shaded.

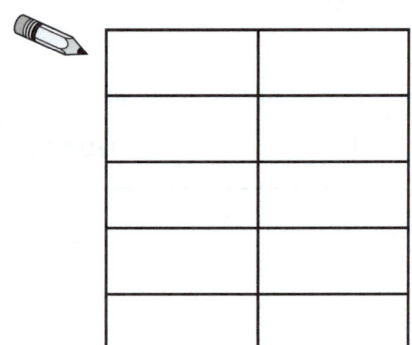

1 mark

3 Shade $\dfrac{9}{10}$ of each of the shapes below.

"Who dares to face me... the evil Count Intenths?"

2 marks

4 $\dfrac{2}{10}$ is marked on the number line below.

Start at $\dfrac{2}{10}$ and count on three tenths. What fraction have you reached?

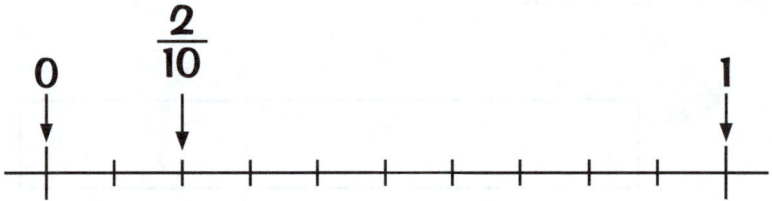

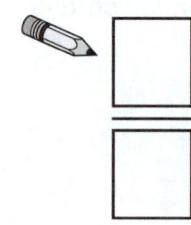

1 mark

Equivalent Fractions

1 Shade the square on the right so that it has the same fraction shaded as the square on the left.

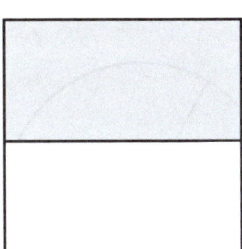  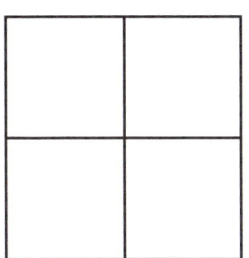

1 mark

2 Tick the circle that is $\frac{1}{4}$ shaded.

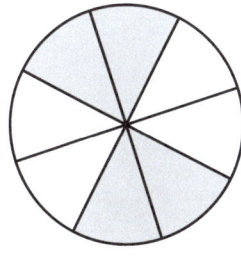 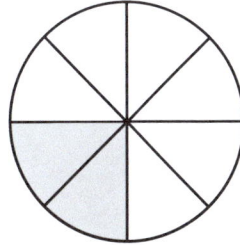 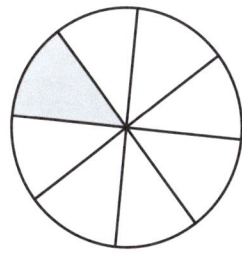

1 mark

3 $\frac{2}{3}$ of the rectangle below is shaded.

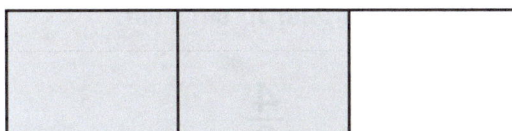

Shade an equivalent fraction of the rectangle below.
Then use it to help you complete the number sentence.

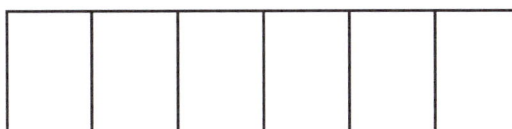   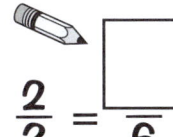

$\frac{2}{3} = \frac{\square}{6}$

2 marks

Section Three — Fractions

Ordering Fractions

1 These two circles have been equally divided.

Shade $\frac{1}{3}$ of the circle below.   Shade $\frac{2}{3}$ of the circle below.

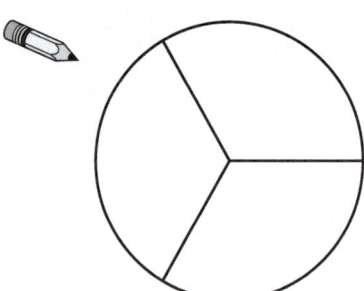 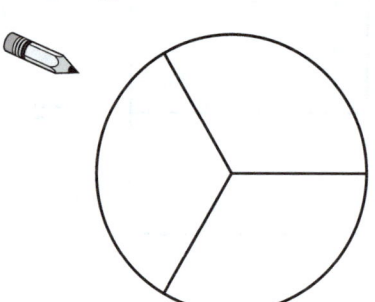

Which fraction is larger, $\frac{1}{3}$ or $\frac{2}{3}$?

2 Circle the smaller fraction in each pair.

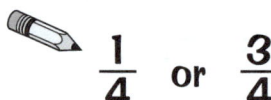 $\frac{1}{4}$ or $\frac{3}{4}$ $\frac{3}{6}$ or $\frac{2}{6}$

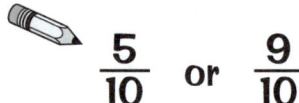 $\frac{5}{10}$ or $\frac{9}{10}$ 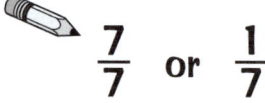 $\frac{7}{7}$ or $\frac{1}{7}$

3 Put these fractions in order from largest to smallest.

$\frac{5}{9}$ $\frac{4}{9}$ $\frac{8}{9}$

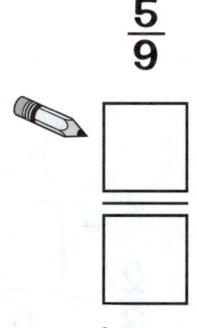   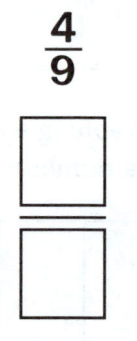   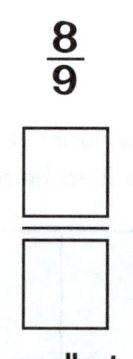

largest   smallest

Ordering Fractions

4 Misty and Solomon are each given identical brownies.

Misty eats $\frac{1}{3}$ of her brownie. Shade $\frac{1}{3}$ of the rectangle below.

1 mark

Solomon eats $\frac{1}{5}$ of his brownie. $\frac{1}{5}$ of the rectangle below has been shaded.

Who has eaten more of their brownie, Misty or Solomon?

1 mark

5 Circle the fraction that is smaller than $\frac{1}{2}$.

$\frac{1}{4}$ $\frac{2}{4}$ $\frac{3}{4}$

1 mark

6 Which of these fractions is the biggest?

Circle your answer.

$\frac{1}{12}$ $\frac{1}{6}$ $\frac{1}{7}$

1 mark

You can use the fraction bars below to help you.

Section Three — Fractions

Adding and Subtracting Fractions

1 Shade the final shape to show the answer to this addition.

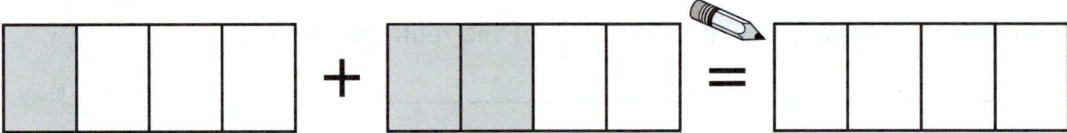

1 mark

2 Fill in the boxes to makes these sums correct.

$\frac{1}{3} + \frac{1}{3} = \frac{\Box}{3}$ $\frac{2}{5} + \frac{1}{5} = \frac{\Box}{5}$

2 marks

3 Shade the final shape to show the answer to this subtraction.

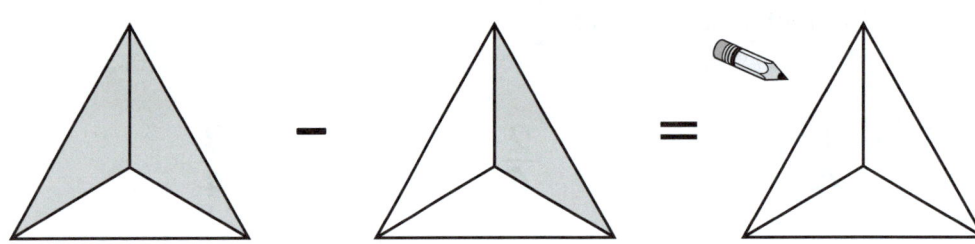

1 mark

4 Match the calculations with their answers.

The first one has been done for you.

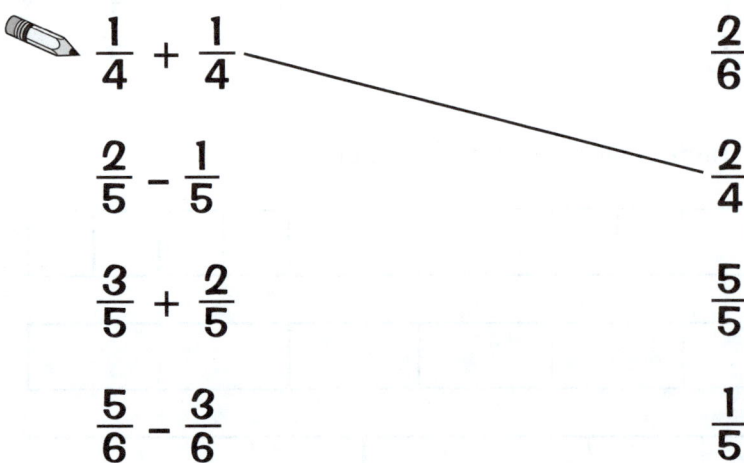

$\frac{1}{4} + \frac{1}{4}$ ———— $\frac{2}{4}$

$\frac{2}{5} - \frac{1}{5}$ $\frac{2}{6}$

$\frac{3}{5} + \frac{2}{5}$ $\frac{5}{5}$

$\frac{5}{6} - \frac{3}{6}$ $\frac{1}{5}$

2 marks

Section Three — Fractions

Adding and Subtracting Fractions

5 What is one sixth plus three sixths?

Write your answer as a fraction.

☐/☐

1 mark

6 Work out the answers to these subtractions.

$\frac{3}{7} - \frac{2}{7} = \frac{\square}{\square}$

1 mark

$\frac{4}{5} - \frac{2}{5} = \frac{\square}{\square}$

1 mark

$1 - \frac{7}{10} = \frac{\square}{\square}$

1 mark

7 Fill in the boxes to make these calculations correct.

$\frac{2}{9} + \frac{\square}{\square} = \frac{7}{9}$ $\frac{\square}{\square} - \frac{2}{4} = \frac{1}{4}$

2 marks

Section Three — Fractions

Fractions of Amounts

1 Five pineapples are shown below.

Circle $\frac{2}{5}$ of the pineapples.

1 mark

2 Fill in the boxes to make the calculations correct.

$\frac{1}{2}$ of 10 = 10 ÷ ☐ 2 ☐ = ☐

1 mark

$\frac{1}{3}$ of 12 = 12 ÷ ☐ = ☐

1 mark

$\frac{1}{4}$ of 20 = 20 ÷ ☐ = ☐

1 mark

3 Circle $\frac{1}{4}$ of the triangles below.

 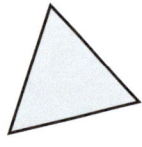    

 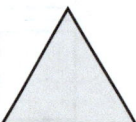    

1 mark

Section Three — Fractions

Fractions of Amounts

4) Eugenie has painted 8 pictures. $\frac{1}{4}$ of the pictures are of the beach.

How many pictures are of the beach?

 pictures

1 mark

How many pictures are <u>not</u> of the beach?

 pictures

1 mark

5) There are 6 pigs below.

What fraction of the pigs are upside down? Circle the correct answer.

$\frac{1}{3}$ $\frac{2}{3}$ $\frac{1}{6}$ $\frac{1}{2}$

1 mark

What is $\frac{2}{3}$ of 6?

1 mark

6) Fill in the boxes below to complete the calculations.

$\frac{1}{4}$ of 20 = 20 ÷ ☐ = ☐ , so

$\frac{3}{4}$ of 20 = 3 × ☐ = ☐

2 marks

Section Three — Fractions

Solving Fraction Problems

1) Leonora has 4 mugs.

What fraction of Leonora's mugs are spotty?

1 mark

What fraction of Leonora's mugs are not spotty?

1 mark

2) Look at the two rectangles below.

Shade $\frac{1}{2}$ of this rectangle.   Shade $\frac{1}{8}$ of this rectangle.

1 mark

A chocolate bar is split into eight equal pieces.
How many pieces would you need to eat to have eaten half the bar?

_____ pieces

1 mark

3) A car is travelling at 50 mph when it overtakes a lorry.
The lorry's speed is $\frac{1}{2}$ that of the car.

What is the lorry's speed?

_____ mph

1 mark

Section Three — Fractions

Solving Fraction Problems

4 A minibus has 12 seats. Pupils are sitting on 5 of the seats and teachers are sitting on 3 of the seats. The rest of the seats are empty.

What fraction of the seats have people sitting on them?

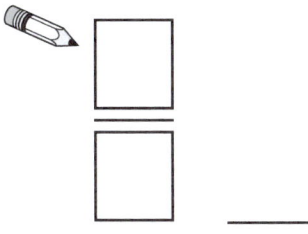

1 mark

5 Chikodi is given £10. He spends $\frac{2}{5}$ of it on an ice cream sundae.

How much did the ice cream sundae cost?

1 mark

6 The fractions show how far three friends have cycled along a bike track.

Phil $\frac{5}{6}$ Molly $\frac{1}{12}$ Lucy $\frac{1}{6}$

Who has cycled the furthest?

1 mark

Lucy cycles another $\frac{3}{6}$ of the track.
What fraction of the track has she now cycled in total?

1 mark

Section Three — Fractions

Length, Mass and Volume

1 Draw a straight line that is 60 mm long in the space below.

1 mark

2 How many millilitres are there in 1 litre?

ml

1 mark

3 Circle the larger measurement.

5 kg   500 g

1 mark

4 April needs 800 g of flour to bake a loaf of bread. She has 300 g of flour.

How much more flour does April need?

g

1 mark

5 Grigor fills two bowls with soup.

475 ml   310 ml

One bowl holds 475 ml of soup.
The other bowl holds 310 ml of soup.

What is the total volume of soup in the two bowls?

ml

1 mark

Section Four — Measurement

Length, Mass and Volume

6 How much taller is tower B than tower A?

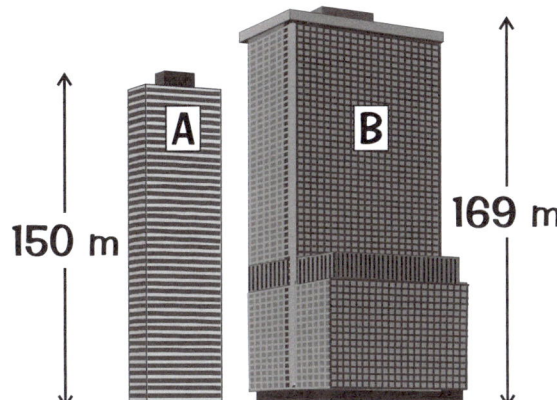

[____] m

1 mark

7 Cement is sold in bags. The weights of three bags are below.

Bag A
2 kg

Bag B
2100 g

Bag C
220 g

Which bag is the heaviest?

[____]

1 mark

8 Roxanne measures a blade of grass. Its length is 55 mm.

Draw an arrow on the ruler to show the length of the blade of grass.

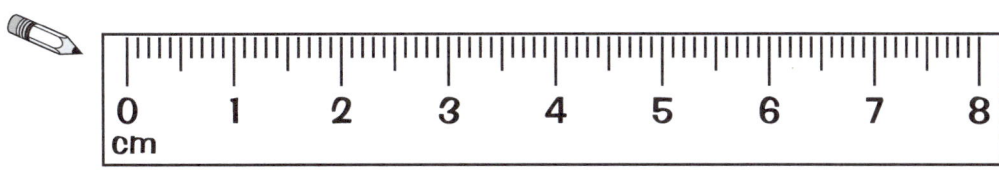

1 mark

A different blade of grass is 2 cm long.
What is the total length of the two blades in millimetres?

[____] mm

1 mark

Section Four — Measurement

Perimeter

1 Work out the perimeter of these shapes.

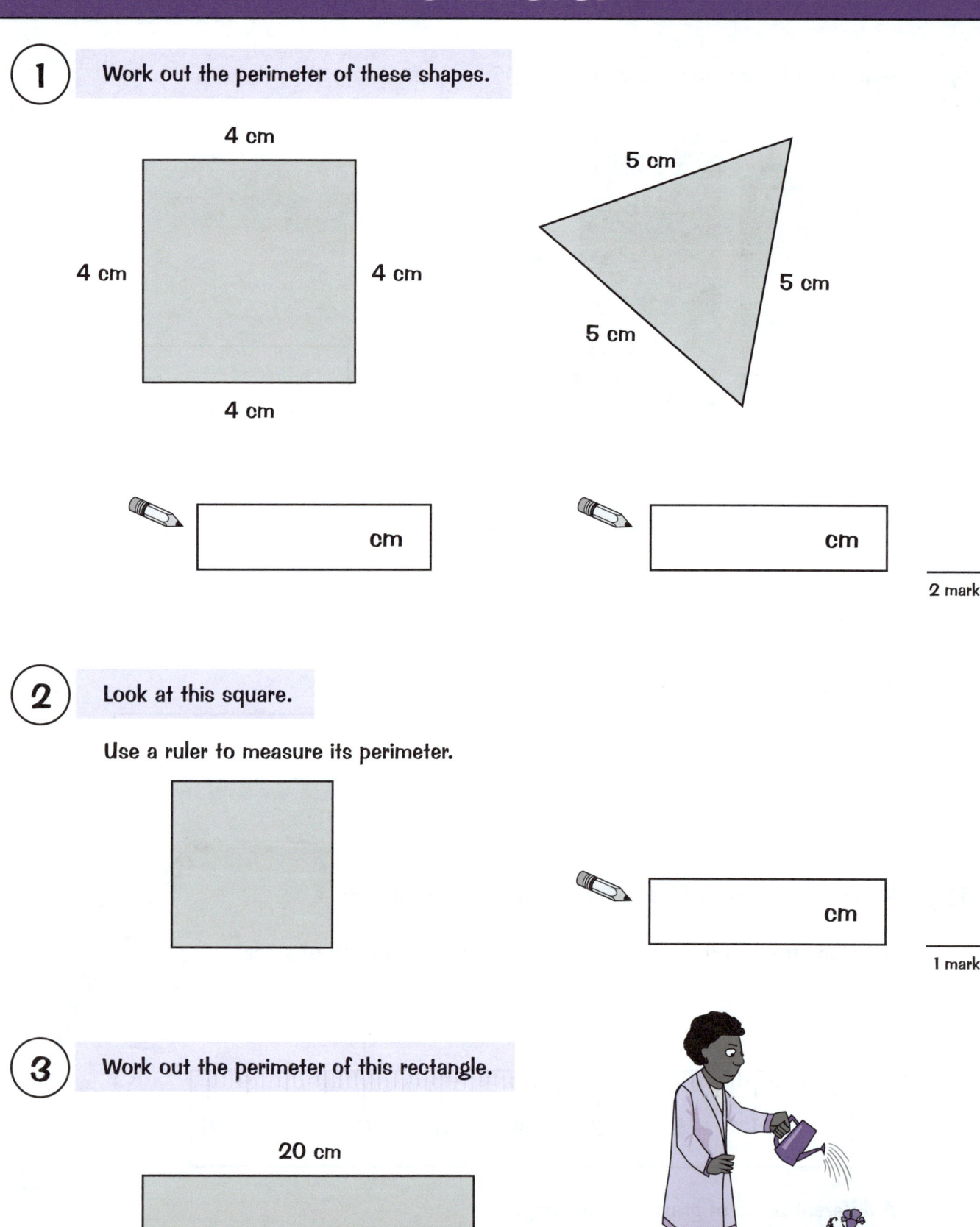

✏️ [   ] cm

✏️ [   ] cm

_____
2 marks

2 Look at this square.

Use a ruler to measure its perimeter.

✏️ [   ] cm

_____
1 mark

3 Work out the perimeter of this rectangle.

✏️ [   ] cm

_____
1 mark

Perimeter

4 The sides of a triangle are 3 cm, 2 cm and 1 cm.

What is the perimeter of the triangle?

[ ] cm

1 mark

5 Use a ruler to measure the perimeter of these shapes.

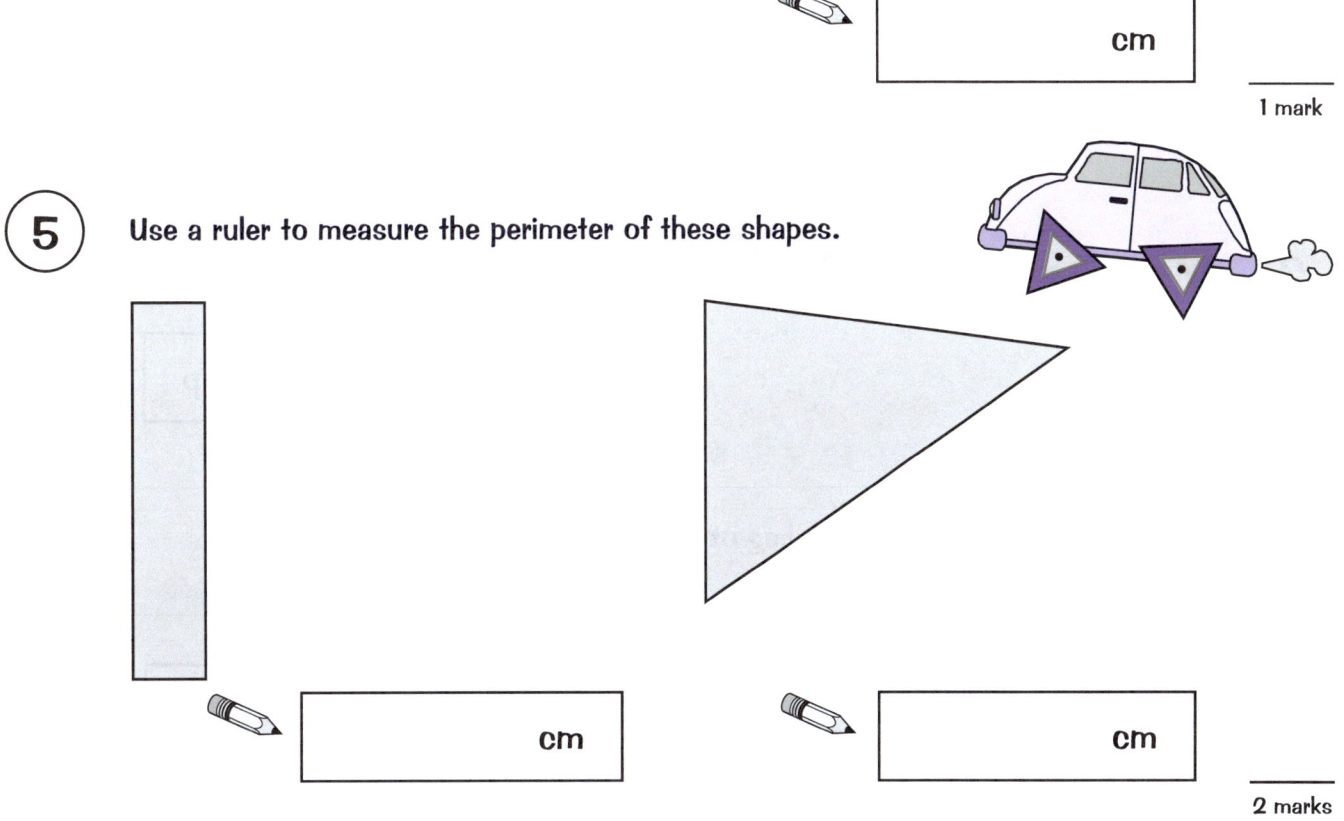

[ ] cm   [ ] cm

2 marks

6 Draw a rectangle with a perimeter of 24 cm on this centimetre square grid.

One side has been done for you.

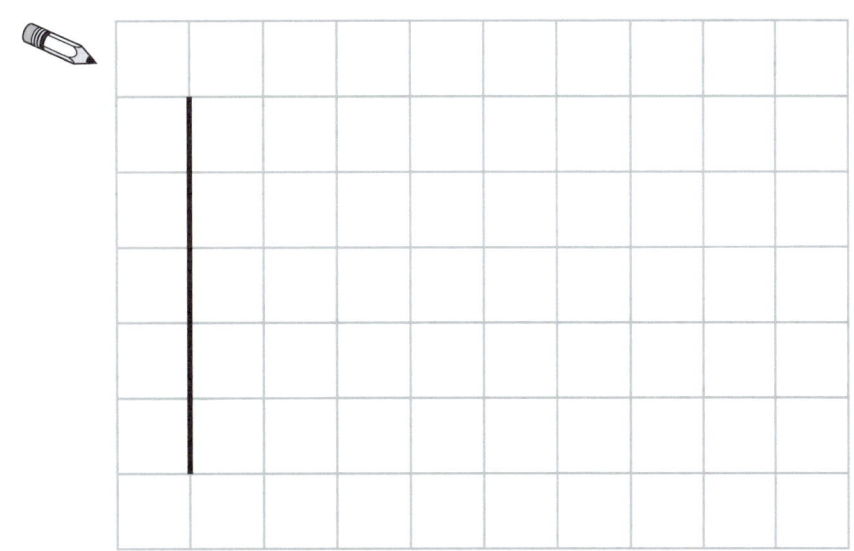

1 mark

Section Four — Measurement

Money

1 Work out:

£40 + £31 = £ ☐

34p + 52p = ☐ p

1 mark

1 mark

2 What is £1 and 25p written all in pence?

☐ p

1 mark

3 Kamal buys a toy for £9 and a bag of sweets for 65p.

How much did he spend in total in pence?

☐ p

1 mark

4 Bev wants to buy this teapot. She has saved up £4 and 50p.

How much more money does she need to buy the teapot?

£ ☐ and ☐ p

1 mark

5 A portion of chips costs £1 and 70p. Drew pays with a £2 coin.

How much change does he get?

☐ p

1 mark

Section Four — Measurement

Clocks

1 Circle the correct number in each sentence.

There are 6 / 31 / 60 / 600 seconds in a minute.

1 mark

There are 24 / 60 / 52 / 366 days in a leap year.

1 mark

2 Write these times in words.

06:30

1 mark

13:25

1 mark

3 Look at these clocks.

A B C D

Write the letter of the clock that shows the time:

quarter past four

1 mark

sixteen minutes to four

1 mark

4 What date is 1 day before 1st April?

1 mark

Section Four — Measurement

Time Problems

1 A game show begins at 15:00.
It finishes at 15:45.

How long is the game show on for?

[_____ minutes]

1 mark

2 Nigel's maths lesson starts at ten past nine and lasts one hour.

When did the maths lesson end?   Write your answer in words.

[_____]

1 mark

3 Gottfried goes to sleep at 11 o'clock at night.
His alarm wakes him up 2 hours later.

Circle the time that he is woken up.

1 am   1 pm   9 am   9 pm

1 mark

4 A plane takes off from Inverness at 11:30.
It lands in London 1 hour and 15 minutes later.

Write the time that the plane lands using the 24-hour clock.

[_____]

1 mark

Section Four — Measurement

Time Problems

5 Brie is on the bus for 30 minutes. She gets off the bus at 09:45.

Draw hands on this watch to show the time that she gets <u>on</u> the bus.

1 mark

6 Here is part of a board shown in a cinema.

Film	Start Time	Finish Time
Illinois!	20:30	22:30
Rain in Leeds	21:00	22:30
Draughts	21:05	

Draughts lasts for 1 hour.
Write the time that it finishes using the 24-hour clock.

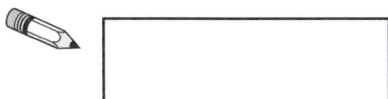

1 mark

How long is *Illinois!* on for?

 hours

1 mark

How much longer is *Illinois!* on for than *Rain in Leeds*?

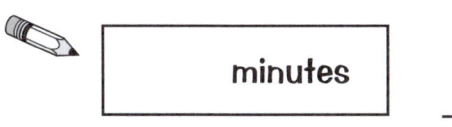 minutes

1 mark

Section Four — Measurement

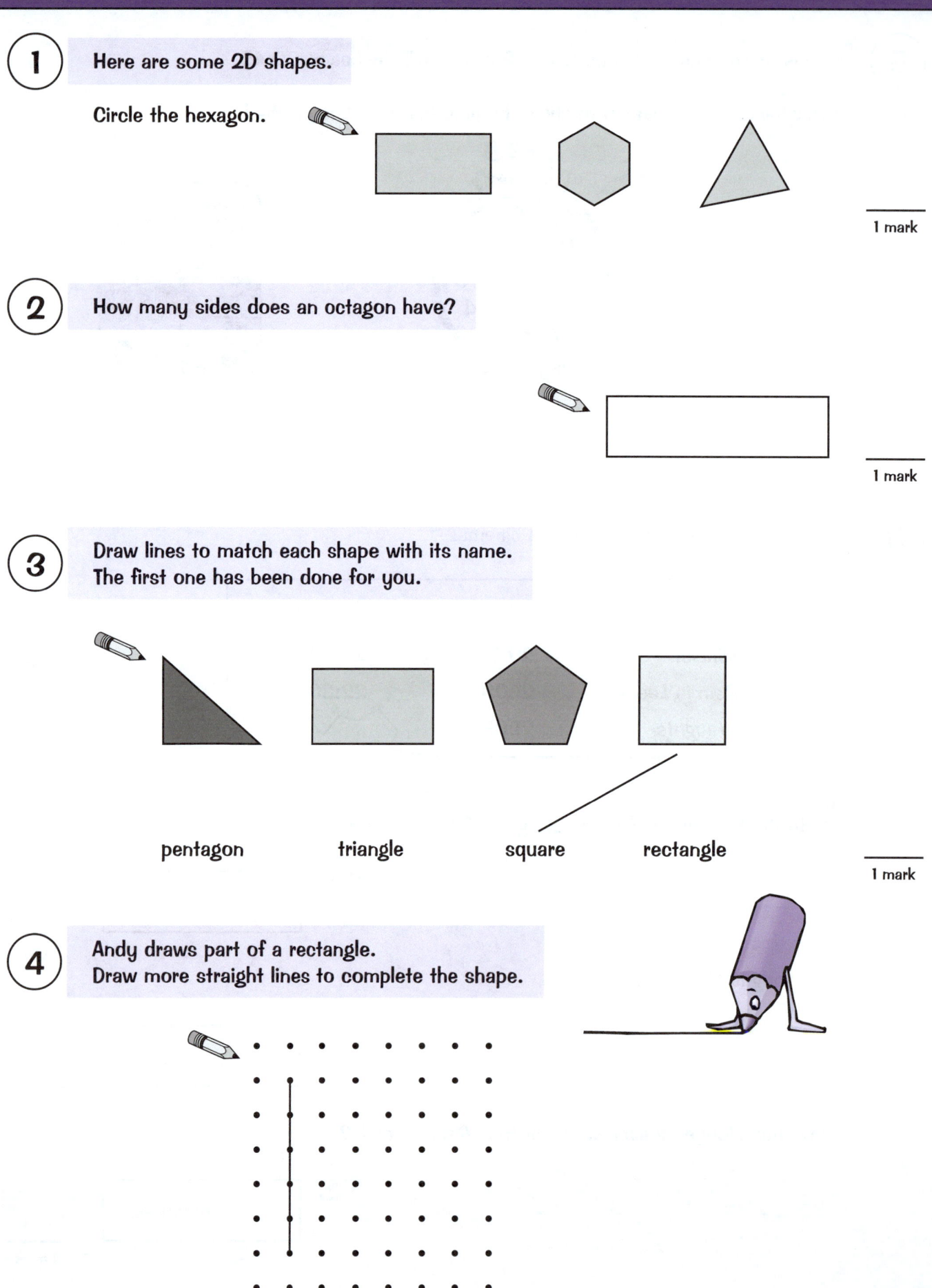

2D Shapes

5 Fill in the boxes with the correct numbers.

A hexagon has [ ] sides and

1 mark

[ ] angles.

1 mark

6 Draw a triangle with one side of 2 cm and one side of 4 cm.
The third side can be any length.

Use a ruler.

1 mark

7 Draw lines to match the start and end of these sentences so that they make sense.

A circle...   ... has five sides that aren't all the same length.

An irregular pentagon...   ... has no corners.

A regular shape...   ... has sides of equal length.

3 marks

Section Five — Geometry

3D Shapes

1) Draw lines to match each 3D shape with its name.

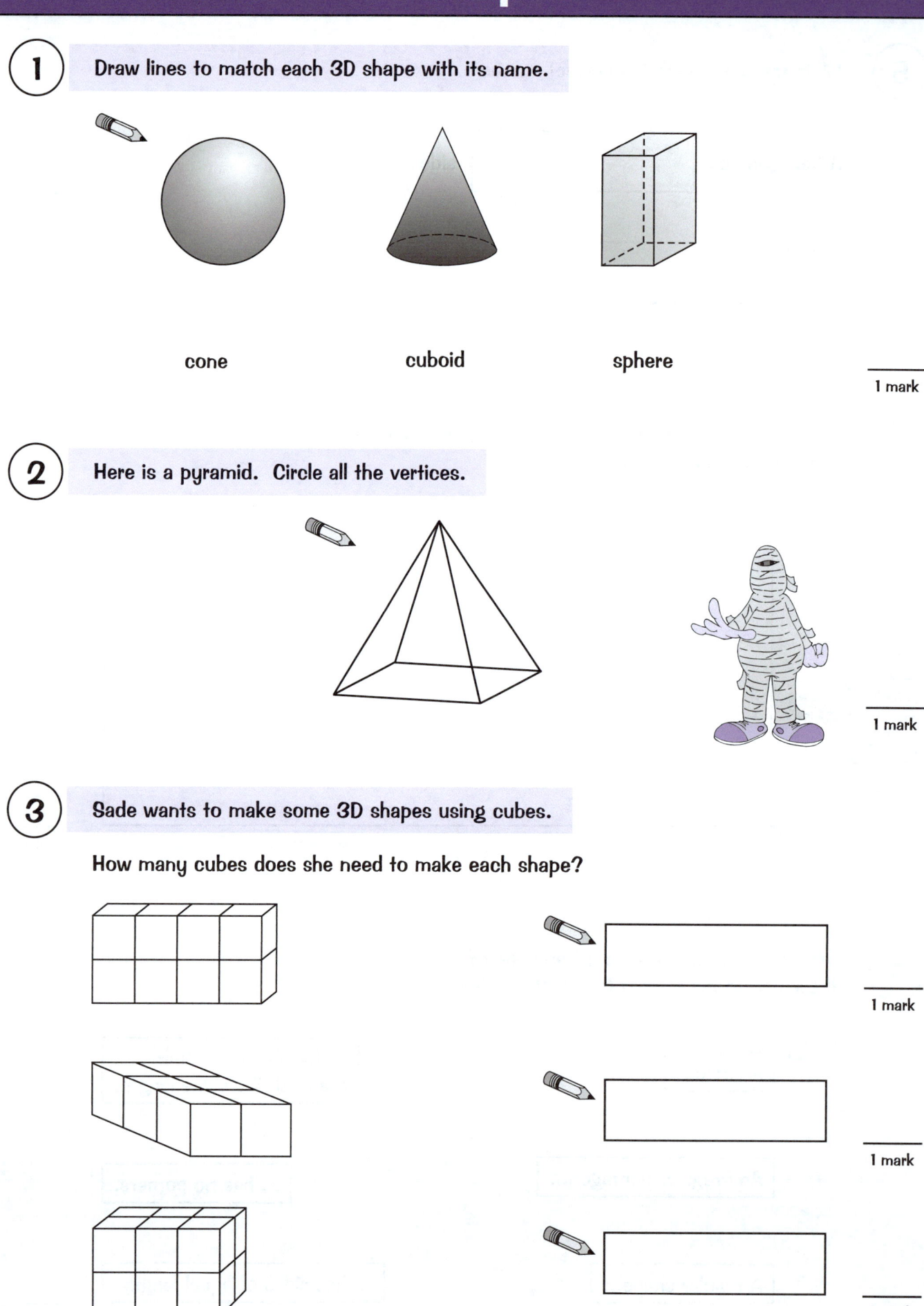

cone   cuboid   sphere

1 mark

2) Here is a pyramid. Circle all the vertices.

1 mark

3) Sade wants to make some 3D shapes using cubes.

How many cubes does she need to make each shape?

1 mark

1 mark

1 mark

Section Five — Geometry

3D Shapes

4 Circle all the shapes that have six faces.

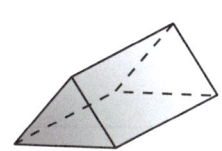 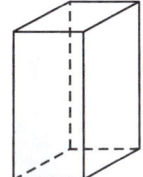 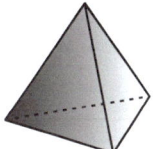 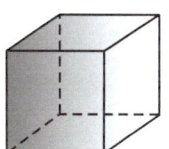

1 mark

5 Here is a hemisphere.

Use two of the words in the box below to fill in the gaps.

| circle | square | sphere | cone |

A hemisphere is half a ☐ .

1 mark

The flat surface of a hemisphere is a ☐ .

1 mark

6 Write down the letters of all the shapes below that are prisms.

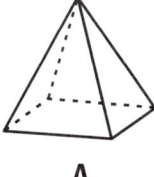   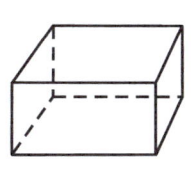   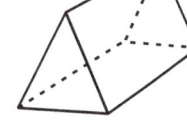   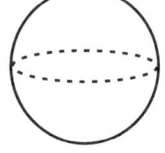

A   B   C   D

1 mark

Section Five — Geometry

Angles and Lines

1) How many right angles are in the shape below?

1 mark

2) Are the angles bigger or smaller than a right angle? Tick the correct box.

☐ bigger ☐ smaller   ☐ bigger ☐ smaller   ☐ bigger ☐ smaller

3 marks

3) James goes to a pet shop. He stands facing the fish tank.

How many right angles clockwise would he need to turn to see the snakes?

1 mark

4) Leena stands in the playground and turns a full circle. She then does another quarter turn.

How many right angles has she turned altogether?

1 mark

Section Five — Geometry

Angles and Lines

5 Circle the pair of lines that are parallel.

1 mark

6 Here is a shape.

How many vertical lines are in this shape?

1 mark

How many horizontal lines are in this shape?

1 mark

7 Fill in the boxes to make the sentences about the rectangle correct.

Side A is parallel to side ☐ .

1 mark

Side B is perpendicular to side ☐ and side ☐ .

1 mark

Section Five — Geometry

Section Six — Statistics

Tables

1 Amal counts the numbers of different insects that she sees on a tree. She puts them in a tally chart.

Insect	Tally
ladybird	卌
butterfly	I
ant	卌 卌 II
beetle	III

Which insect did she see the most?

1 mark

How many ladybirds were there?

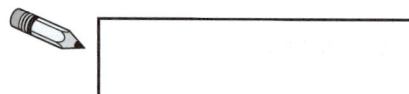

1 mark

2 Frank wants to make a tally chart of all his toys.

Use the picture to fill in the tally chart.

Toy	Tally	Total
doll	III	3
car		
plane		

2 marks

3 Bertrand makes a tally chart of the objects on his school desk.

Complete his table below.

Object	Tally	Total
books		3
pens	I	
coloured pencils	卌 III	

2 marks

Bar Charts

1 This bar chart shows the different colours of mugs in a kitchen cupboard.

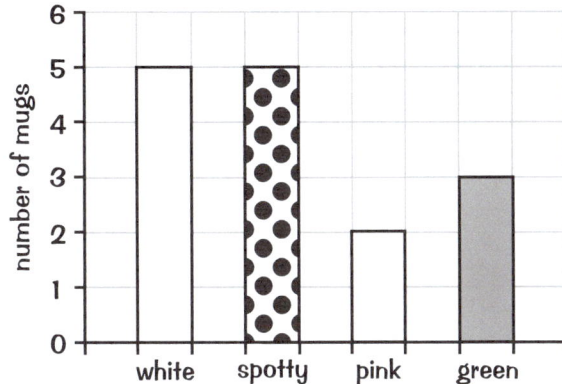

How many spotty mugs are there?

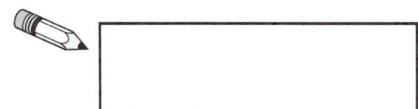

1 mark

How many pink mugs are there?

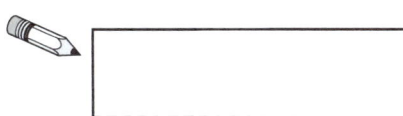

1 mark

2 Isla buys a bag of sweets from the shop. She counts out the different sweets. Some of them are shown in the bar chart.

She has 6 rosy apples and 10 cola bottles.
Use this information to complete the bar chart.

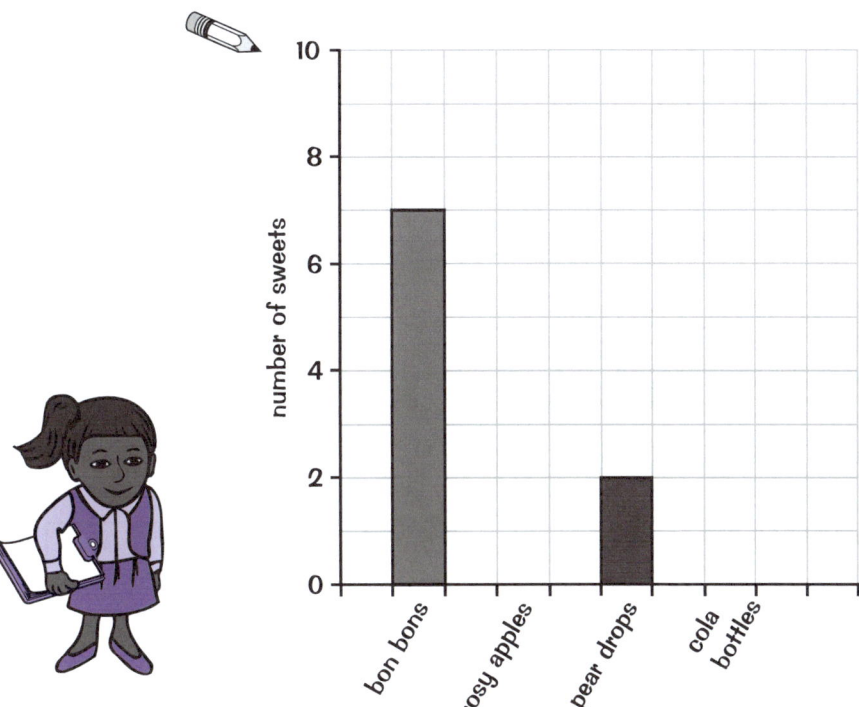

1 mark

How many bon bons and pear drops are there altogether?

1 mark

Section Six — Statistics

Pictograms

1) Azi wants to fill her house with plants.
She buys some new plants each day.

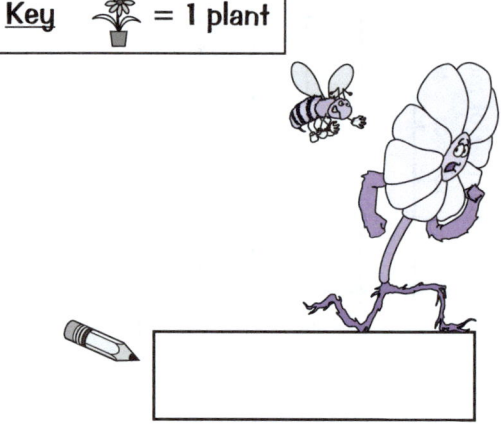

How many plants did she buy on Monday?

1 mark

How many plants did she buy altogether on Wednesday and Thursday?

1 mark

2) Farid records the number of each type of sandwich in a sandwich shop.

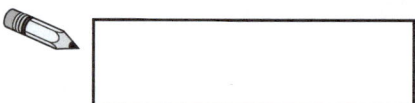

How many ham sandwiches are there?

1 mark

How many tuna sandwiches are there?

1 mark

There are 4 cheese sandwiches.
Add this to the pictogram.

1 mark

Section Six — Statistics

Interpreting Tables and Charts

1) This bar chart shows the number of drinks sold at a stall.

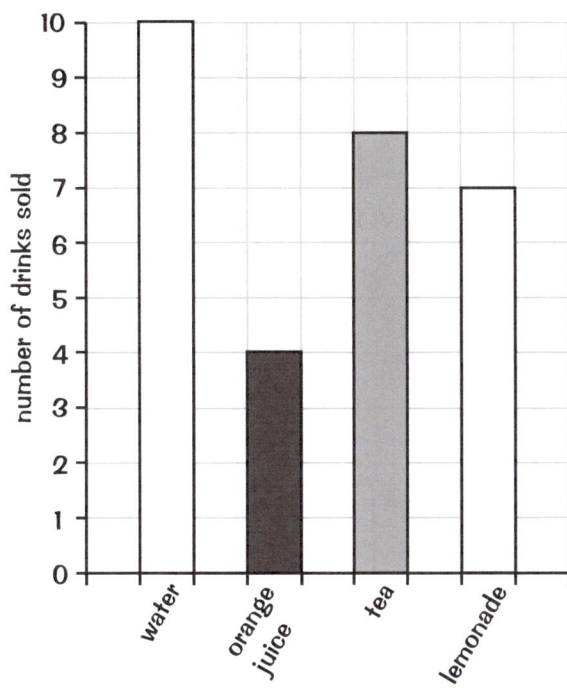

What is the total number of drinks sold?

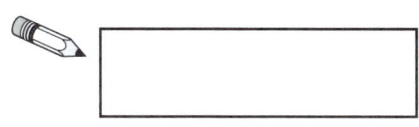

1 mark

How many more waters were sold than teas?

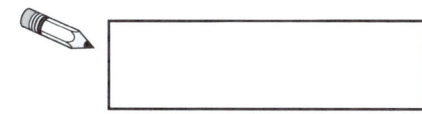

1 mark

2) Four friends collected some shells from a beach.
The number of shells they collected is shown in the pictogram below.

Harry	🐚 🐚 🐚 🐚
Ruby	🐚 🐚 🐚 🐚 🐚
Sean	🐚 🐚
Maria	🐚 🐚 🐚

Key 🐚 = 2 shells

How many more shells did Ruby collect than Sean?

1 mark

How many shells did Harry and Maria collect altogether?

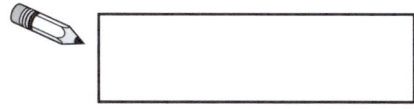

1 mark

Section Six — Statistics

Year Three Objectives Test

1) Put these numbers in order. Start with the smallest.

   247   **614**   **254**

   [smallest]   [ ]   [largest]

   1 mark

2) Write two hundred and ninety two in digits.

   [ ]

   1 mark

3) Look at the shape below.

   Shade $\frac{5}{6}$ of the shape.

   Write down the name of the shape.

   [ ]

   1 mark

4) Circle all the numbers with a 5 in the 'tens' place.

   556   458   514   975

   1 mark

5) How many minutes are there between 13:05 and 13:40?

   [ ] minutes

   1 mark

Year Three Objectives Test

6) Circle the name of this 3D shape.

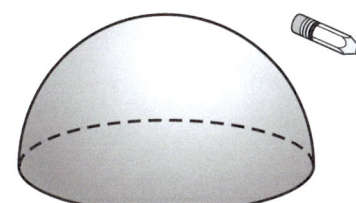
        hemisphere   cube

        cylinder   pyramid

1 mark

7) The bar chart shows the numbers of workers in a shop on different days.

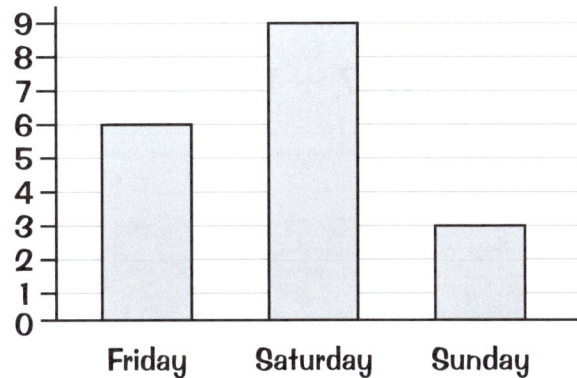

Which day has the most workers?

1 mark

How many more workers were there on Saturday than Sunday?

 workers

1 mark

8) Fill in the boxes to make these calculations correct.

 × 4 = 24   × 4 = 240

2 marks

Year Three Objectives Test

Year Three Objectives Test

9) A barrel contains 150 litres of oil.

Radeyah pours out 40 litres of oil.
How much oil is left in the barrel?

☐ litres

1 mark

10) Calculate:

957 − 421   347 + 136

☐   ☐

2 marks

11) A child bus fare costs £2.
An adult bus fare costs £3 and 50p.

How much do two child bus fares cost?
Circle the correct answer.

550p   400p   200p   350p

1 mark

Bruno pays the adult bus fare with a £5 note.
How much change does he get?

£ ☐ and ☐ p

1 mark

Year Three Objectives Test

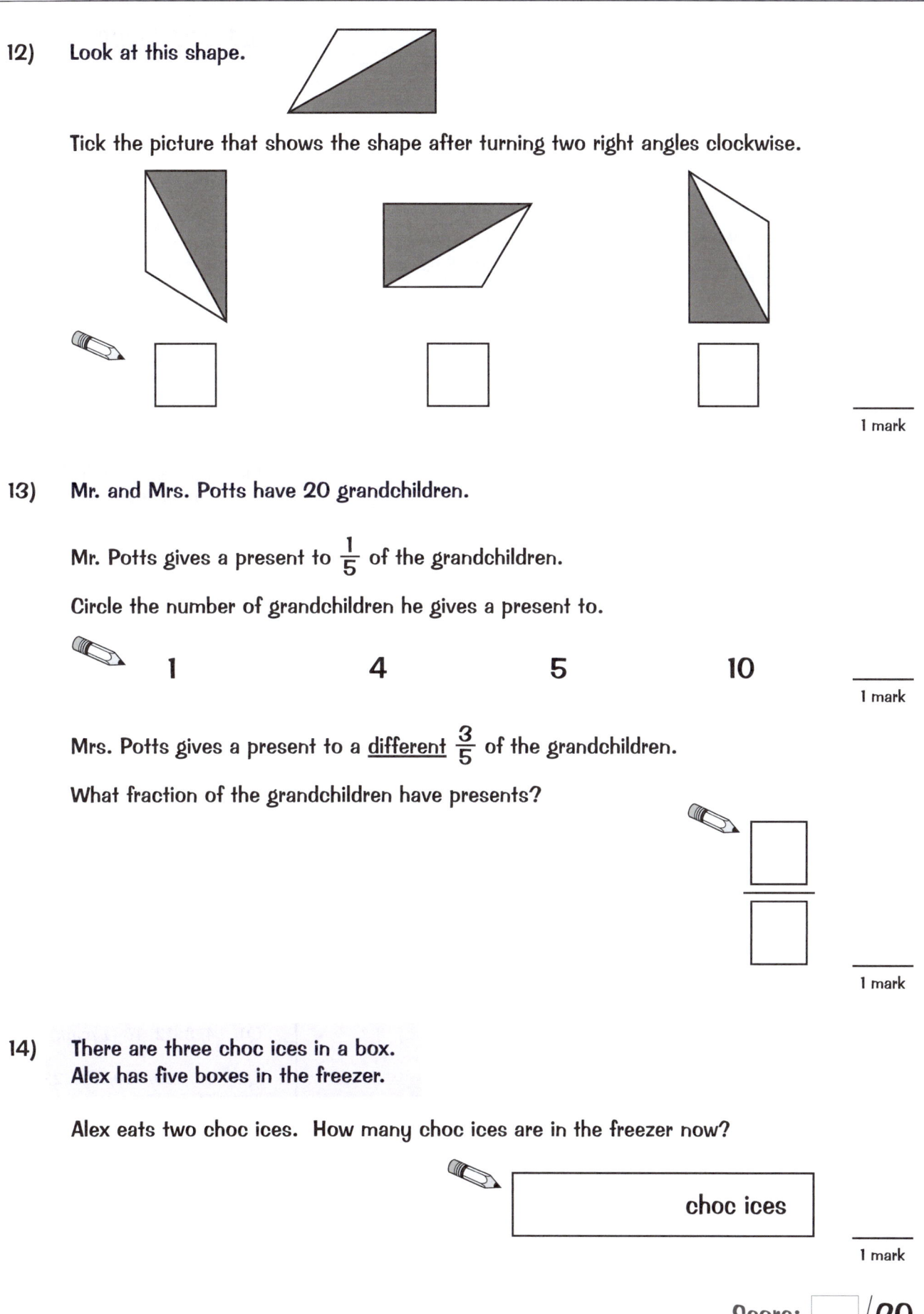

12) Look at this shape.

Tick the picture that shows the shape after turning two right angles clockwise.

1 mark

13) Mr. and Mrs. Potts have 20 grandchildren.

Mr. Potts gives a present to $\frac{1}{5}$ of the grandchildren.

Circle the number of grandchildren he gives a present to.

1   4   5   10

1 mark

Mrs. Potts gives a present to a <u>different</u> $\frac{3}{5}$ of the grandchildren.

What fraction of the grandchildren have presents?

1 mark

14) There are three choc ices in a box.
Alex has five boxes in the freezer.

Alex eats two choc ices. How many choc ices are in the freezer now?

_____ choc ices

1 mark

Score: ___ /20

Answers

Pages 2-5 – Year Two Objectives Test

Q1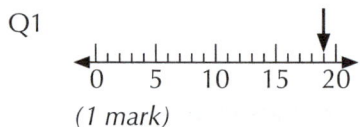
(1 mark)

Q2 **8** (1 mark)

Q3 **140 g < 150 g** (1 mark)

Q4 **33 shells** (1 mark)

Q5 These shapes should be ticked:
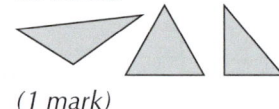
(1 mark)

Q6 **90** and **81** (1 mark)

Q7 **Text message** (1 mark)
5 (1 mark)

Q8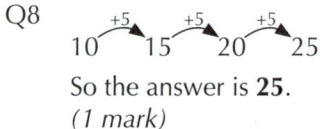
So the answer is **25**.
(1 mark)

Q9 8 × 2 = **16** (1 mark)
5 × 10 = **50** (1 mark)

Q10 48 + 6 = **54 classes** (1 mark)
48 − 10 = **38 classes** (1 mark)

Q11 **Quarter past seven** (1 mark)

Q12 **B** (1 mark)

Q13 5 + 8 + 2 = **15** (1 mark)

Q14 The shapes and words should be matched up like this:

 6 square faces

 0 vertices and 2 edges

 0 vertices and 0 edges

 5 vertices and 5 faces

(2 marks for all correct, 1 mark for one or two correct)

Q15 $\frac{1}{4}$ (1 mark)
$\frac{1}{2}$ (1 mark)

Section One – Number and Place Value

Page 6 – Place Value

Q1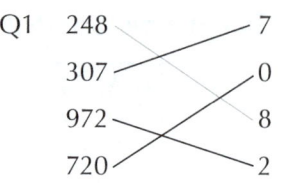

(2 marks for all correct, 1 mark for one or two correct)

Q2 **2** (1 mark)

Q3 **8** (1 mark)
3 (1 mark)

Q4 The 4 in 412 is in the **hundreds** place. (1 mark)

Q5 **60** or **6 tens** (1 mark)

Page 7 – Reading and Writing Numbers

Q1 **959** (1 mark)
715 (1 mark)

Q2 **103** (1 mark)

Q3 **eight hundred and forty six** (1 mark)

Q4 **three hundred and sixty two** (1 mark)

Page 8 – Counting in Multiples

Q1 4, **8**, 12, 16 (1 mark)

Q2 50, 100, **150**, **200**, **250** (1 mark)

Q3 **8**, **16**, 24, **32**, 40 (1 mark)

Q4 **200**, **300**, **900** (1 mark)

Q5 40, **48**, 56 (1 mark)

Answers

Page 9 – 10 or 100 More or Less

Q1 **61** *(1 mark)*

Q2 **324** *(1 mark)*

Q3 **640** *(1 mark)*

Q4 **800** *(1 mark)*

Q5 **99** *(1 mark)*

Q6 870, 880, **890**, 900, **910** *(1 mark)*

Pages 10-11 – Ordering and Comparing Numbers

Q1 **702** *(1 mark)*

Q2 **349** *(1 mark)*

Q3 578 is **smaller** than 590. *(1 mark)*
    421 is **larger** than 321. *(1 mark)*

Q4 **102, 191, 380** *(1 mark)*

Q5 **850, 320, 111, 56** *(1 mark)*

Q6 981 **>** 891 *(1 mark)*

Q7 **167 g** *(1 mark)*

Q8 68 is smaller than 97 and 301 so **Camilla** has the fewest coins. *(1 mark)*

Q9 **224 < 250** *(1 mark)*

Pages 12-13 – Partitioning

Q1 220 = 200 + **20** *(1 mark)*
    309 = **300** + 9 *(1 mark)*
    870 = 800 + **70** *(1 mark)*

Q2 500 + 80 = **580** *(1 mark)*
    100 + 60 + 1 = **161** *(1 mark)*

Q3 542 = 500 + **40** + **2** *(1 mark)*
    468 = **400** + 60 + **8** *(1 mark)*
    951 = **900** + **50** + 1 *(1 mark)*

Q4 617 = **600** + **10** + **7** *(1 mark)*
    999 = **900** + **90** + **9** *(1 mark)*

Q5 E.g. **20 + 7** *(1 mark)*
    E.g. **100 + 10 + 2** *(1 mark)*
    27 + 112
    = 20 + 7 + 100 + 10 + 2
    = 100 + 30 + 9 = **139**
    (1 mark)

Q6 E.g.
    100 + 80 + 4 + 10 + 3
    = 100 + 90 + 7 = **197**
    (2 marks — 1 mark for an attempt at partitioning, 1 mark for the correct answer)

Q7 500 + 30 + 2 = **532** *(1 mark)*

Pages 14-15 – Numbers on Scales

Q1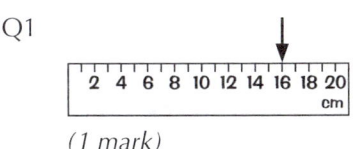
    (1 mark)

Q2 **50 °C** *(1 mark)*

Q3 **40 mm** *(1 mark)*

Q4
    (1 mark)

Q5 **8 litres** *(1 mark)*

Q6 **90 cm** *(1 mark)*

Q7 **350 g** *(1 mark)*

Pages 16-17 – Solving Number Problems

Q1 **150** *(1 mark)*

Q2 **200 + 50 + 1** *(1 mark)*
    Beachville *(1 mark)*

Q3 **150 pennies** *(1 mark)*

Q4 **£386** *(1 mark)*

Q5 300 + 10 + 9
    = **319 metres** *(1 mark)*

Q6 8 + 8 + 8 + 8 = **32 °C** *(1 mark)*

Answers

Section Two – Calculations

Page 18 – Mental Addition

Q1 456 + 2 = **458** *(1 mark)*
671 + 5 = **676** *(1 mark)*
202 + 9 = **211** *(1 mark)*

Q2 231 + 50 → 281
330 + 20 → 350
518 + 80 → 598
128 + 70 → 198
(2 marks for all correct, 1 mark for one or two correct)

Q3 462 + 500 = **962** *(1 mark)*
148 + 800 = **948** *(1 mark)*

Q4 564 + **7** = 571 *(1 mark)*
219 + **201** = 420 *(1 mark)*

Page 19 – Mental Subtraction

Q1 845 – 3 = **842** *(1 mark)*
158 – 5 = **153** *(1 mark)*
747 – 8 = **739** *(1 mark)*

Q2 905 – 100 → 805
455 – 300 → 155
558 – 500 → 58
875 – 700 → 175
(2 marks for all correct, 1 mark for one or two correct)

Q3 265 – 20 = **245** *(1 mark)*
754 – **30** = 724 *(1 mark)*

Q4 751 – 40 = **711** *(1 mark)*

Page 20 – Written Addition

Q1
```
  2 6 4
+   3 4
  2 9 8
```
(1 mark)

```
  3 2 1
+   5 8
  3 7 9
```
(1 mark)

```
  4 7 3
+ 1 2 4
  5 9 7
```
(1 mark)

```
  2 2 8
+ 7 2 1
  9 4 9
```
(1 mark)

Q2
```
  8 4 7
+ 1 2 7
  9 7 4
    ¹
```
(1 mark)

Q3
```
  7 8 5
+   4 3
  8 2 8
  ¹
```
So **828 steps** *(1 mark)*

Page 21 – Written Subtraction

Q1
```
  8 4 5
–   1 1
  8 3 4
```
(1 mark)

```
  6 8 7
–   7 4
  6 1 3
```
(1 mark)

```
  8 5 9
– 3 4 6
  5 1 3
```
(1 mark)

```
  2 7 4
– 2 3 1
      4 3
```
(1 mark)

Q2
```
  3 ⁵6̸ ¹4
– 1 5 9
  2 0 5
```
(1 mark)

Q3
```
  ³4̸ ¹2 6
– 2 8 6
  1 4 0
```
(1 mark)

Page 22 – The 3, 4 and 8 Times Tables

Q1 4 + 4 + 4
= 3 × 4 = **12** *(1 mark)*
8 + 8 + 8 + 8 + 8
= **5** × 8 = **40** *(1 mark)*

Q2 3 × 3 = **9** *(1 mark)*
6 × 4 = **24** *(1 mark)*
11 × 8 = **88** *(1 mark)*

Q3 **8** × 8 = 64 *(1 mark)*
5 × **4** = 20 *(1 mark)*

Q4 In nine days, the cat takes
9 × 4 = **36 naps**. *(1 mark)*

Answers

Pages 23-24 – Using Times Tables Facts

- **Q1** $5 \times 3 = 15$
  so $15 \div 3 = \mathbf{5}$ *(1 mark)*
  $7 \times 4 = 28$
  so $28 \div 7 = \mathbf{4}$ *(1 mark)*

- **Q2** $8 \times 7 = 7 \times 8 = \mathbf{56}$ *(1 mark)*
  $7 \times 80 = \mathbf{560}$ *(1 mark)*
  $70 \times 8 = \mathbf{560}$ *(1 mark)*

- **Q3** $3 \times 6 = \mathbf{18}$ *(1 mark)*
  $30 \times 6 = \mathbf{180}$ *(1 mark)*

- **Q4**
  $30 \times 8 \longrightarrow 160$
  $4 \times 40 \longrightarrow 480$
  $6 \times 80 \longrightarrow 240$
  $20 \times 3 \longrightarrow 60$
  (2 marks for all correct, 1 mark for one or two correct)

- **Q5** $9 \times 4 = 36$
  so $36 \div 4 = \mathbf{9}$ *(1 mark)*
  $360 \div 4 = \mathbf{90}$ *(1 mark)*

- **Q6** $9 \div 3 = 3$
  so $90 \div 3 = 30$
  So they make **30 jumpers** each. *(1 mark)*

- **Q7** $20 \times 2 = \mathbf{40}$
  $4 \times 2 = \mathbf{8}$
  So 24×2
  $= 40 + 8 = \mathbf{48}$ *(1 mark)*

  $10 \times 4 = \mathbf{40}$
  $7 \times 4 = \mathbf{28}$
  So 17×4
  $= 40 + 28 = \mathbf{68}$ *(1 mark)*

- **Q8** E.g. $48 = 30 + 18$
  $= 10 \times 3 + 6 \times 3$
  $= 16 \times 3$
  So $48 \div 3 = \mathbf{16}$ *(1 mark)*

Page 25 – Estimating and Checking

- **Q1** $27 + 57 = 84$
  or $57 + 27 = 84$ *(1 mark)*

- **Q2** $15 \times \mathbf{3} = 45$ *(1 mark)*

- **Q3** $\mathbf{10 + 30}$ *(1 mark)*

- **Q4** $\mathbf{100 \div 5}$ *(1 mark)*
  E.g. $100 \div 5 = \mathbf{20}$, which is not close to 40. *(1 mark)*

Pages 26-27 – Solving Calculation Problems

- **Q1** $280 - 60 = \mathbf{220}$ **trains** *(1 mark)*

- **Q2**
  ```
    1 4 6
  +   3 3
  ───────
    1 7 9
  ```
  So there are **179 children**. *(1 mark)*

- **Q3** $4 \times 3 = \mathbf{12}$ **crayons** *(1 mark)*

- **Q4**
  ```
    3 4 2
  + 4 3 9
  ───────
    7 8 1
        ₁
  ```
  (1 mark)

- **Q5** $6 \div 3 = 2$, so $60 \div 3 = 20$.
  So there are **20 trees** in each park. *(1 mark)*

- **Q6** $12 \times 8 = \mathbf{96}$ **cabbages** *(1 mark)*
  $16 \div 8 = \mathbf{2}$ **boxes** *(1 mark)*

- **Q7** $2 \times 4 = \mathbf{8}$ **letters** *(1 mark)*
  $5 \times 4 = 20$ so she posts her 20th letter on the fifth day. This is **Friday**. *(1 mark)*

Section Three – Fractions

Page 28 – Counting in Tenths

- **Q1** $1 \div 10 = \dfrac{1}{10}$ *(1 mark)*
  $6 \div 10 = \dfrac{6}{10}$ *(1 mark)*

- **Q2**
  (1 mark)

- **Q3** E.g.
  (1 mark)

  E.g.
  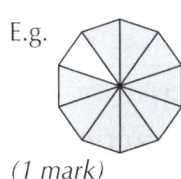
  (1 mark)

- **Q4** Counting up in tenths:
  $\dfrac{2}{10} \to \dfrac{3}{10} \to \dfrac{4}{10} \to \dfrac{5}{10}$
  So the answer is $\dfrac{\mathbf{5}}{\mathbf{10}}$.
  (1 mark)

Answers

Page 29 – Equivalent Fractions

Q1 E.g.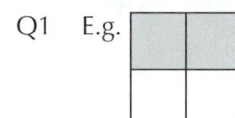
(1 mark)

Q2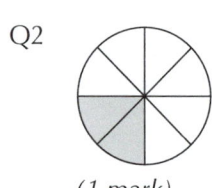
(1 mark)

Q3 E.g. ▭▭▭▭▭▭
(1 mark)

$\frac{2}{3} = \frac{\mathbf{4}}{6}$ (1 mark)

Pages 30-31 – Ordering Fractions

Q1 E.g.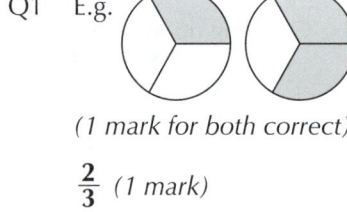
(1 mark for both correct)

$\frac{\mathbf{2}}{\mathbf{3}}$ (1 mark)

Q2 $\frac{\mathbf{1}}{\mathbf{4}}, \frac{\mathbf{2}}{\mathbf{6}}, \frac{\mathbf{5}}{\mathbf{10}}$ and $\frac{\mathbf{1}}{\mathbf{7}}$
(2 marks for all correct, 1 mark for three correct)

Q3 $\frac{\mathbf{8}}{\mathbf{9}}, \frac{\mathbf{5}}{\mathbf{9}}, \frac{\mathbf{4}}{\mathbf{9}}$ (1 mark)

Q4 E.g. ▭▭▭
(1 mark)

Comparing the rectangles, $\frac{1}{3} > \frac{1}{5}$.
So **Misty** has eaten more.
(1 mark)

Q5 $\frac{\mathbf{1}}{\mathbf{4}}$ (1 mark)

Q6 $\frac{\mathbf{1}}{\mathbf{6}}$ (1 mark)

Pages 32-33 – Adding and Subtracting Fractions

Q1 E.g.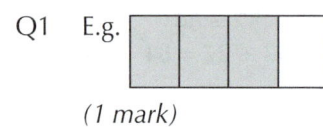
(1 mark)

Q2 $\frac{1}{3} + \frac{1}{3} = \frac{1+1}{3} = \frac{\mathbf{2}}{\mathbf{3}}$
(1 mark)

$\frac{2}{5} + \frac{1}{5} = \frac{2+1}{5} = \frac{\mathbf{3}}{\mathbf{5}}$
(1 mark)

Q3 E.g.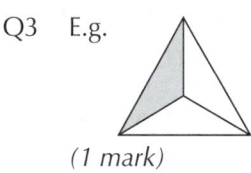
(1 mark)

Q4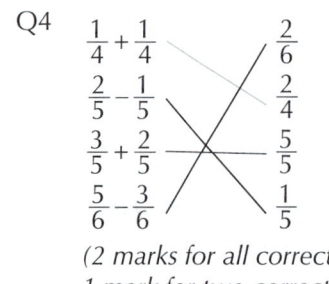
(2 marks for all correct, 1 mark for two correct)

Q5 $\frac{1}{6} + \frac{3}{6} = \frac{\mathbf{4}}{\mathbf{6}}$ or $\frac{\mathbf{2}}{\mathbf{3}}$
(1 mark)

Q6 $\frac{3}{7} - \frac{2}{7} = \frac{\mathbf{1}}{\mathbf{7}}$ (1 mark)

$\frac{4}{5} - \frac{2}{5} = \frac{\mathbf{2}}{\mathbf{5}}$ (1 mark)

$1 - \frac{7}{10} = \frac{10}{10} - \frac{7}{10}$
$= \frac{\mathbf{3}}{\mathbf{10}}$ (1 mark)

Q7 $\frac{2}{9} + \frac{5}{9} = \frac{\mathbf{7}}{\mathbf{9}}$ (1 mark)

$\frac{3}{4} - \frac{2}{4} = \frac{\mathbf{1}}{\mathbf{4}}$ (1 mark)

Pages 34-35 – Fractions of Amounts

Q1 E.g.
(1 mark)

Q2 $\frac{1}{2}$ of $10 = 10 \div 2 = \mathbf{5}$
(1 mark)

$\frac{1}{3}$ of $12 = 12 \div \mathbf{3} = \mathbf{4}$
(1 mark)

$\frac{1}{4}$ of $20 = 20 \div \mathbf{4} = \mathbf{5}$
(1 mark)

Q3 E.g. ◁△▽△◁▽
△△△△◁▷
(1 mark)

Q4 $\frac{1}{4}$ of $8 = 8 \div 4 = \mathbf{2}$
So **2 pictures** are of the beach. (1 mark)

$8 - 2 = \mathbf{6}$
So **6 pictures** are not of the beach. (1 mark)

Q5 $\frac{\mathbf{1}}{\mathbf{3}}$ (1 mark)

4 (1 mark)

Q6 $\frac{1}{4}$ of $20 = 20 \div \mathbf{4} = \mathbf{5}$
(1 mark),

so $\frac{3}{4}$ of $20 = 3 \times \mathbf{5} = \mathbf{15}$.
(1 mark)

Answers

Pages 36-37 – Solving Fraction Problems

Q1 $\frac{1}{4}$ are spotty *(1 mark)*
    $\frac{3}{4}$ aren't spotty *(1 mark)*

Q2 E.g.
    (1 mark for both correct)
    You would need to eat **4 pieces**. *(1 mark)*

Q3 $\frac{1}{2}$ of 50 = 50 ÷ 2
    = **25 mph** *(1 mark)*

Q4 There are 5 + 3 = 8 occupied seats out of a total of 12 seats.
    So $\frac{8}{12}$ or $\frac{2}{3}$ of the seats have people sitting on them. *(1 mark)*

Q5 $\frac{1}{5}$ of £10 = £10 ÷ 5 = £2
    $\frac{2}{5}$ of £10 = 2 × £2
    = **£4** *(1 mark)*

Q6 $\frac{5}{6}$ is greater than $\frac{1}{6}$.
    $\frac{1}{6}$ is greater than $\frac{1}{12}$.
    So **Phil** has cycled the furthest. *(1 mark)*
    Lucy has now cycled $\frac{1}{6} + \frac{3}{6} = \frac{4}{6}$ or $\frac{2}{3}$ of the track. *(1 mark)*

Section Four – Measurement

Pages 38-39 – Length, Mass and Volume

Q1 A straight line should be drawn measuring 60 mm. Allow 59-61 mm. *(1 mark)*

Q2 **1000 ml** *(1 mark)*

Q3 5 × 1000 = 5000 g
    So **5 kg** is larger. *(1 mark)*

Q4 800 – 300 = **500 g** *(1 mark)*

Q5 475 + 300 = 775
    775 + 10 = 785
    So 475 + 310 = **785 ml** *(1 mark)*

Q6 169 – 150 = **19 m** *(1 mark)*

Q7 Bag A weighs 2 × 1000 = 2000 g
    So **Bag B** is the heaviest. *(1 mark)*

Q8 *(1 mark)*
    2 cm = 20 mm
    20 + 55 = **75 mm** *(1 mark)*

Pages 40-41 – Perimeter

Q1 4 + 4 + 4 + 4 = **16 cm** *(1 mark)*
    5 + 5 + 5 = **15 cm** *(1 mark)*

Q2 3 + 3 + 3 + 3 = **12 cm** *(1 mark)*

Q3 20 + 5 + 20 + 5 = **50 cm** *(1 mark)*

Q4 3 + 2 + 1 = **6 cm** *(1 mark)*

Q5 1 + 5 + 1 + 5 = **12 cm** *(1 mark)*
    4 + 5 + 6 = **15 cm** *(1 mark)*

Q6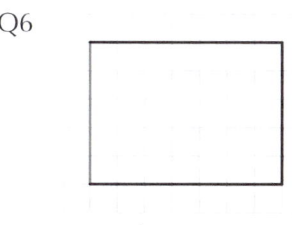
    (1 mark)

Page 42 – Money

Q1 40 + 31 = **£71** *(1 mark)*
    34 + 50 = 84
    84 + 2 = 86
    So 34 + 52 = **86p** *(1 mark)*

Q2 £1 + 25p
    100 + 25
    = **125p** *(1 mark)*

Q3 £9 + 65p
    900 + 65
    = **965p** *(1 mark)*

Q4 £4 and 50p = 450p
    600 – 400 = 200
    200 – 50 = 150p
    = **£1 and 50p** *(1 mark)*

Q5 £1 and 70p = 170p
    200 – 100 = 100
    100 – 70 = **30p** *(1 mark)*

Answers

Page 43 – Clocks

Q1 **60** *(1 mark)*
366 *(1 mark)*

Q2 **half past six** *(1 mark)*
twenty-five past one
(1 mark)

Q3 quarter past four **D**
(1 mark)
sixteen minutes to four **B**
(1 mark)

Q4 **31st March** *(1 mark)*

Pages 44-45 – Time Problems

Q1 **45 minutes** *(1 mark)*

Q2 **ten past ten** *(1 mark)*

Q3 11 pm to 12 am = 1 hour.
12 am + 1 hour = 1 am.
1 am should be circled.
(1 mark)

Q4 11:30 + 1 hour = 12:30.
12:30 + 15 mins = **12:45**
(1 mark)

Q5 9:45 – 30 mins = 9:15

(1 mark)

Q6 21:05 + 1 hour = **22:05**
(1 mark)

2 hours *(1 mark)*

Rain in Leeds is on for
1 hour and 30 minutes so
Illinois! is **30 minutes** longer.
(1 mark)

Section Five – Geometry

Pages 46-47 – 2D Shapes

Q1
(1 mark)

Q2 **8** *(1 mark)*

Q3 The shapes and names should be matched up like this:

 triangle

 rectangle

 pentagon

(1 mark for all correct)

Q4 E.g.

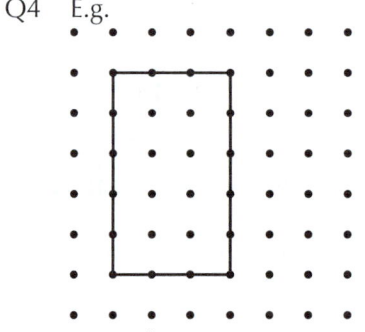

(1 mark)

Q5 **6** *(1 mark)*
6 *(1 mark)*

Q6 E.g.
2 cm
4 cm
(1 mark)

Q7 A circle has no corners.
(1 mark)

An irregular pentagon has
five sides that aren't all the
same length. *(1 mark)*

A regular shape has sides of
equal length. *(1 mark)*

Pages 48-49 – 3D Shapes

Q1 The shapes and names should be matched up like this:

 sphere

 cone

 cuboid

(1 mark for all correct)

Q2

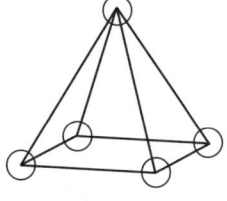

(1 mark)

Q3 **8** *(1 mark)*
6 *(1 mark)*
12 *(1 mark)*

Q4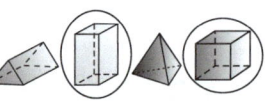
(1 mark)

Q5 **sphere** *(1 mark)*
circle *(1 mark)*

Q6 **B** and **C** *(1 mark)*

Answers

Pages 50-51 – Angles and Lines

Q1 **3** *(1 mark)*

Q2 **bigger** *(1 mark)*
smaller *(1 mark)*
smaller *(1 mark)*

Q3 **2** right angles *(1 mark)*

Q4 **5** turns *(1 mark)*

Q5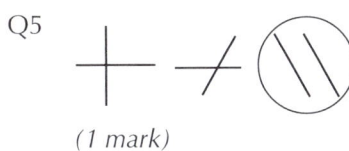
(1 mark)

Q6 **3** *(1 mark)*
1 *(1 mark)*

Q7 **C** *(1 mark)*
A and **C** *(1 mark)*

Section Six – Statistics

Page 52 – Tables

Q1 **ant** *(1 mark)*
5 *(1 mark)*

Q2

Toy	Tally	Total
doll	|||	3
car	|||| ||	**7**
plane	||	**2**

(2 marks — 1 mark for the car row filled in correctly, 1 mark for the plane row filled in correctly)

Q3

Object	Tally	Total
books	|||	3
pens			**1**
coloured pencils	|||| |||	**8**

(2 marks for all correct, 1 mark for two correct)

Page 53 – Bar Charts

Q1 **5** *(1 mark)*
2 *(1 mark)*

Q2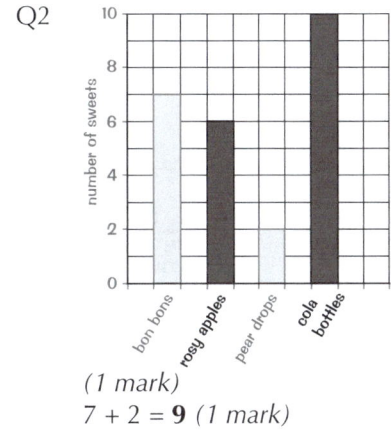
(1 mark)
7 + 2 = **9** *(1 mark)*

Page 54 – Pictograms

Q1 **3** *(1 mark)*
2 + 4 = **6** *(1 mark)*

Q2 4 × 2 = **8** *(1 mark)*
3 × 2 = **6** *(1 mark)*

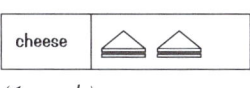

(1 mark)

Page 55 – Interpreting Tables and Charts

Q1 10 + 4 + 8 + 7 = **29**
(1 mark)
10 – 8 = **2** *(1 mark)*

Q2 Ruby collected
5 × 2 = 10 shells.
Sean collected
2 × 2 = 4 shells.
So Ruby collected
10 – 4 = **6** more shells.
(1 mark)

Harry collected
4 × 2 = 8 shells.
Maria collected
3 × 2 = 6 shells.
So they collected
8 + 6 = **14** shells altogether.
(1 mark)

Answers

Pages 56-59 – Year Three Objectives Test

Q1 **247**, **254**, **614** *(1 mark)*

Q2 **292** *(1 mark)*

Q3 E.g.
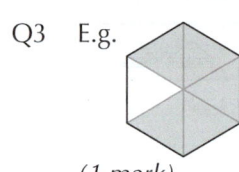
(1 mark)

hexagon *(1 mark)*

Q4 **556** and **458** should be circled. *(1 mark)*

Q5 Count on from 13:05:
13:05 → 13:10 → 13:40
= 5 mins + 30 mins
= **35 minutes** *(1 mark)*

Q6 **hemisphere** *(1 mark)*

Q7 **Saturday** *(1 mark)*
9 – 3 = **6 workers** *(1 mark)*

Q8 **6** × 4 = 24 *(1 mark)*
60 × 4 = 240 *(1 mark)*

Q9 150 – 40 = 110
So there are **110 litres** left in the barrel. *(1 mark)*

Q10
```
  9 5 7
– 4 2 1
  5 3 6
```
(1 mark)

```
  3 4 7
+ 1 3 6
  4 8 3
      1
```
(1 mark)

Q11 200 + 200 = 400
= **400p** *(1 mark)*
£3 and 50p = 350p
500 – 300 = 200
200 – 50 = 150p
So he gets **£1 and 50p** change. *(1 mark)*

Q12
(1 mark)

Q13 **4** *(1 mark)*
$\frac{1}{5} + \frac{3}{5} = \frac{4}{5}$ *(1 mark)*

Q14 5 × 3 = 15
15 – 2 = **13 choc ices**
(1 mark)